SECRET CITIES OF
ITALY

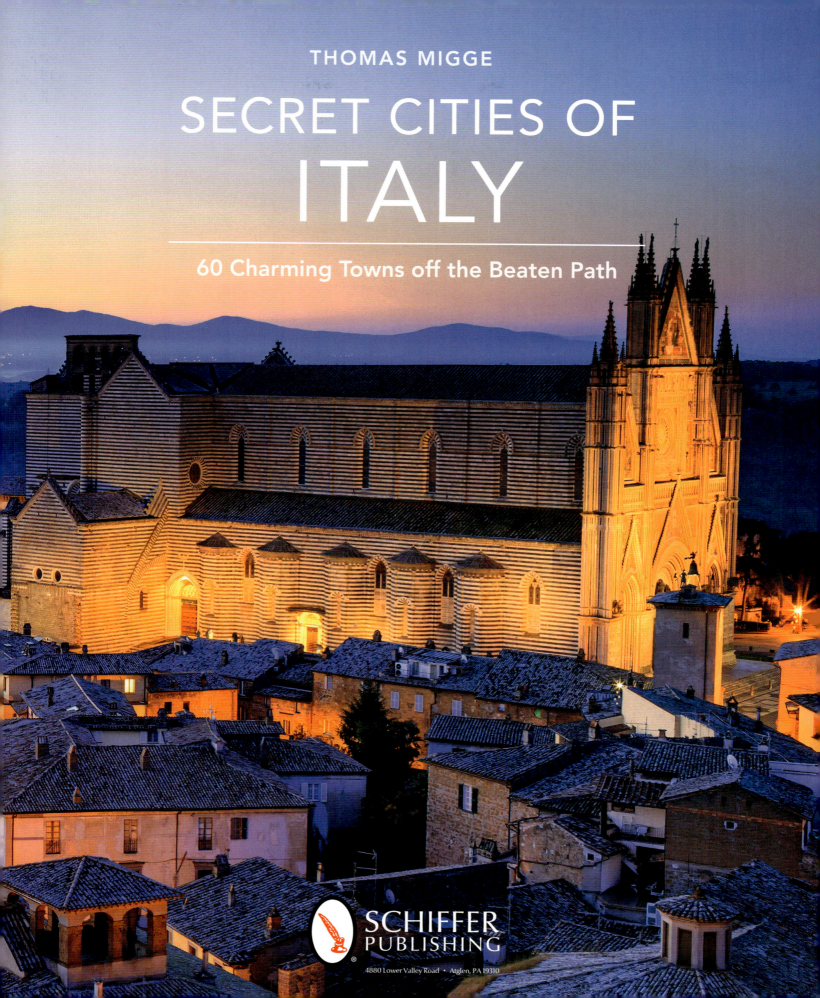

TABLE OF CONTENTS

SECRET CITIES OF ITALY – Revelations for Explorers	8
NORTHERN ITALY	**10**
1 **GLURNS** – The Proud Town in the Mountains	12
2 **AOSTA** – The Wild and Romantic Mountain Resort	14
3 **ORTA SAN GIULIO** – Hidden in the Mountains	16
4 **COMO** – The Small Town by a Picturesque Lakeside	18
5 **BASSANO DEL GRAPPA** – The High-Proof Delight	20
6 **AQUILEIA** – The Mighty Bishop's See	22
7 **BRESCIA** – A World Heritage Town in a Prime Location	24
8 **TREVISO** – Mainland Venice in Miniature	26
9 **TORCELLO** – The Dreamy Island	28
10 **TURIN** – The Cool Classic	30
11 **PAVIA** – Spiritual Greatness and Simple Beauty	34
12 **MANTUA** – The Favorite of the House of Gonzaga	36
13 **MONTAGNANA** – The Walled-In Wonder	42
14 **PARMA** – Something for the Eyes, the Ears, and the Palate	44
15 **FERRARA** – Emilia-Romagna for Romantics	48
16 **POMPOSA** – The Hidden Abbey	52
17 **GENOA** – The Bypassed Metropolis	54
18 **BOLOGNA** – The Great Unknown	60
19 **RAVENNA** – The Imperial City	66
20 **TRIORA** – A Village Idyll in Liguria's Mountains	70
CENTRAL ITALY	**72**
21 **ORSIGNA** – The Elective Home of Tiziano Terzani	74
22 **LA VERNA** – A Place for Holy Legends	76
23 **URBINO** – Treasure Trove in the Marches	78
24 **MONTERIGGIONI** – The Round Miracle	82
25 **GUBBIO** – Strolling through the Middle Ages	84
26 **SAN GALGANO** – Mysterious Middle Ages	88
27 **GIARDINO SPOERRI** – A Garden Full of Ideas	90
28 **SPOLETO** – A Festival Makes History	94
29 **PITIGLIANO** – Italy's Jerusalem	98
30 **ORVIETO** – A First-Class Destination	100
31 **CIVITA DI BAGNOREGIO** – A Village in a Top Location	104

HISTORICAL TOWN CENTERS, QUAINT LITTLE STORES, VILLAGES ATOP ROCKY CLIFFS AND FISHING PORTS, CASTLES, AND STREETS BUSTLING WITH RESTAURANTS: THESE LITTLE-KNOWN CORNERS OF ITALY ARE OFF THE BEATEN TOURIST PATH YET VERY MUCH WORTH EXPLORING.

32 **BOMARZO** – A Fantastical Spot in the Country   106

33 **TUSCANIA** – Lazio's Bright North   108

34 **TARQUINIA** – A Cemetery with an Adjacent Small Town   110

35 **CAPRAROLA** – A Mannerist Manifesto   112

36 **SAN CLEMENTE** – The National Monument   114

37 **ROME UNDERGROUND** – A Very Different Eternal City   116

38 **PALESTRINA** – Built within a Temple   122

39 **OSTIA ANTICA** – Pompeii Vibes   124

40 **NINFA** – Visiting a Magic Garden   128

SOUTHERN ITALY   130

41 **CASERTA** – The Largest Castle in the World   132

42 **TRANI** – Cathedral by the Sea   136

43 **NAPLES** – Italy's Most Fascinating City   138

44 **HERCULANEUM** – Pompeii in Miniature   144

45 **PAESTUM** – Exquisite Doric Temples   148

46 **MATERA** – A Cozy Cave System   150

47 **MARTINA FRANCA** – A Stylish Old Town   152

48 **LECCE** – The Zenith of Architecture   154

49 **OTRANTO** – Puglia's Magical South   156

50 **DIAMANTE** – The Perfect Seaside Resort   158

51 **THARROS** – The Anchorage of Antiquity   160

52 **BARUMINI** – A World Heritage Site in Nature   162

53 **STROMBOLI** – A Great Island Spectacle   164

54 **PALERMO** – The Underestimated City   166

55 **MONREALE** – Dipped in Gold   172

56 **CEFALÙ** – A Charming Old Town by the Sea   176

57 **AGRIGENTO** – A Classic of Antiquity by the Sea   178

58 **PIAZZA ARMERINA** – A Villa Causes a Sensation   180

59 **SYRACUSE** – From Poorhouse to Precious City   182

60 **NOTO** – Risen from the Ashes   186

INDEX   190

PHOTO CREDITS   191

CALTANISSETTA IN SICILY: THE ONLY STAIRCASE IN ITALY WITH STEPS ENTIRELY EMBELLISHED WITH HANDMADE TILES.

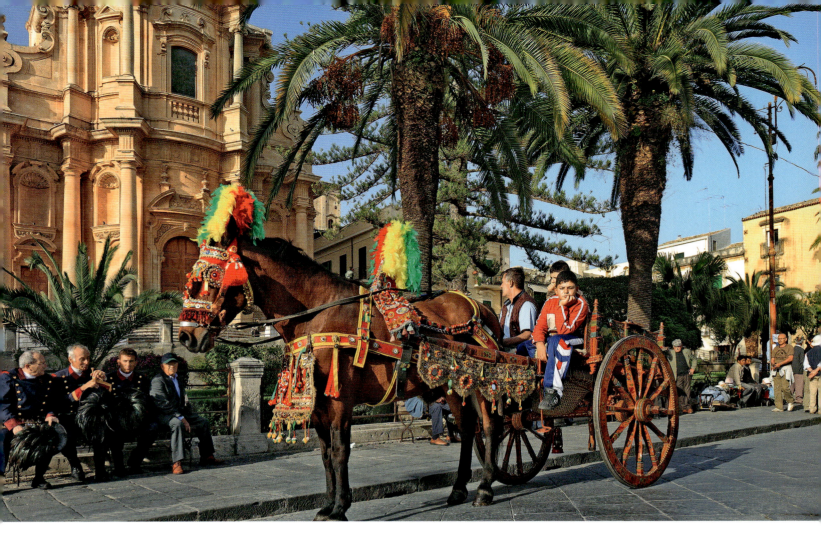

SECRET CITIES OF ITALY
REVELATIONS FOR EXPLORERS

Rome, Venice, Florence: travelers who only ever aim to visit these fascinating Italian cities will certainly see a lot—but they will also miss out on a whole lot more. They will never discover the multitude of other attractive towns and villages in Italy that are waiting to be explored. Instead of being overrun by mass tourism, these spots are brimming with charm—even Italy connoisseurs are in for a surprise!

Bella Italia: beautiful Italy, the land where the lemon trees bloom, in the words of German poet Goethe, has been a popular vacation destination for tourists from all over the globe—and there is indeed a great deal to see and explore. In beach resorts such as Rimini and Forte dei Marmi, you can soak up the sun in style, while Italy's towns and villages also allow you to immerse yourself in history and culture, ranging from antiquity to the baroque era.

Italy is an open book, you may think, as images come to mind of gondolas in Venice, St. Peter's Basilica and the Trevi Fountain in Rome, and Michelangelo's *David* in Florence. There is probably no other European travel destination that has to contend with quite as many opinions and prejudices as Italy. And yet, foreign tourists often only have a faint idea of the multiple faces the Mediterranean country has to offer.

Italy's diverse cities are a case in point. The majority of tourists only visit very few places: Rome, Florence, and Venice, above all. These cities burst at the seams during the high season—which is most of the year. They are so crammed that Venice has

OPPOSITE: **IN NOTO, LIKE IN ALL OF SICILY, THE TRADITION OF DECORATING HORSE CARTS IN BRIGHT COLORS IS STILL ALIVE.** *LEFT:* **THE MUSEO CIVICO IN THE NORTHERN ITALIAN TOWN OF BASSANO DEL GRAPPA HAS OLD AND NEW ART ON DISPLAY.** *BELOW:* **GORGEOUS FRESCOES ADORN THE PALAZZO FARNESE IN THE CENTRAL ITALIAN TOWN OF CAPRAROLA.**

started charging tourists for entry and introducing daily quotas for tourists. Meanwhile in Rome, police officers have to direct the crowds around the Trevi Fountain. The Vatican Museums and the Uffizi Gallery in Florence are so crowded on many days that you can hardly see the art for the people.

A DETOUR INTO THE UNKNOWN

But there is a completely different side to Italy as well: one hardly (or not at all) exploited by tourism. Parts of Italy where visitors are treated with respect because they are individual travelers and not part of a huge group, where not everything is in the service of mass production.

You are spoiled for choice among Italy's "Secret Cities"—these hidden places that are often not even a long drive away from the most famous spots. Never more than one or two hours from the main highways of mass tourism, there are villages, towns, and small and large cities waiting to be discovered. And they are every bit as fascinating as the top Italian destinations. They are places to discover, places to immerse yourself, places to fully experience, and places to simply to enjoy.

But why make the trip to visit Turin or Bologna in the north, or to explore Civita di Bagnoregio and Caprarola in Central Italy, or to discover Noto or Otranto in the south? Who even knew that beneath the much-visited Italian capital lies an entire underground city that can easily compete with the fascinating sites that aboveground Rome has to offer?

DESTINATIONS THAT GO STRAIGHT TO THE HEART

There are about as many guidebooks to Italy as there are Italian tourists. But most of these tomes simply repeat the same old places, missing out on entire regions that some travel guide publishers

consider only marginally or not at all. Often omitted are regions boasting towns full of secrets with palaces, remote abbeys, and rock-hewn churches that make the heart of every Italy traveler beat faster—especially since you don't even have to share them with a lot of people.

This book presents sixty rather less-visited places. Some of these are large cities, such as Naples, with its close to one million inhabitants; others are tiny villages, such as those on the island of Stromboli; and yet others have long ceased to be cities and all that is left are ruins. This book takes a look at sixty special places throughout Italy. In many cases, they can be easily reached by car or train from the main destinations. Or, as in the case of Rome, you simply need to go underground. It is often worth spending at least one night in these spots to experience their charm. *Secret Cities of Italy* is your guarantee to discovering the places hardly any other guidebook will tell you about.

THE VIEW FROM A BAROQUE PALACE TERRACE
TOWARDS THE HUGE HARBOR OF GENOA

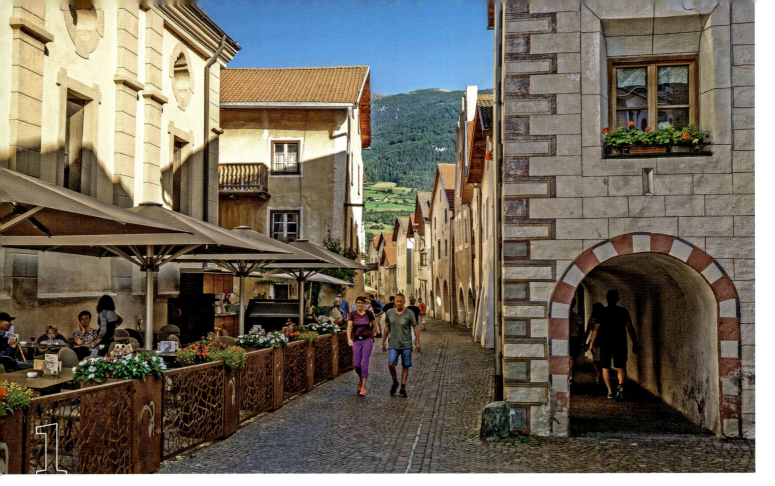

GLURNS – THE PROUD TOWN IN THE MOUNTAINS

THE PAST WITHIN ONE'S REACH

There is no other town in South Tyrol that exudes quite as much old-fashioned charm as Glurns. The pearl of the Vinschgau Valley is one of the smallest towns in the Alps and is particularly attractive in the snow or at night, when you feel transported to the set of a historical movie.

The ancient Romans settled here because of the town's special location. They built a trade route, the Via Claudia Augusta, to transport goods to what is now Switzerland and France and back. But it was not until the Middle Ages that Glurns became a settlement of note. In Italian, the town is called Glorenza; under fascism in Italy, German place names in South Tyrol were typically translated into Italian.

GUARDED BY WALLS

Enjoy a pleasant walk around the almost intact walls of the town, which is at an altitude of approximately 2,950 feet (900 meters). Walls don't come thicker than these: at 27 feet (8 meters) high, they are 5 feet (1.5 meters) thick. The fortified towers, as you can see them today, were erected in the mid-sixteenth century. You still enter Glurns through one of three historical town gates.

Although it boasts neither world-class art nor exceptional architecture, the town itself is an important historical monument—and can be explored and enjoyed on foot in half a day, including lunch or dinner, plus an aperitif or cappuccino. The street of archways from 1499 is a must-see for every visitor.

The parish church Saint Pankratius from 1481, just outside the town walls toward the Adige (or the Etsch) River, is also worth a visit. The church's

OPPOSITE: **GLURNS IS ONE OF NORTHERN ITALY'S BEST-PRESERVED MEDIEVAL TOWNS.**
LEFT: **ITS SURROUNDINGS CAN BE EASILY EXPLORED ON FOOT OR BY BIKE.**

baroque onion dome can be spotted from afar. Inside, it houses a large fresco from the late fifteenth century depicting the Last Supper in minute detail. Further pieces of sacred art were also lovingly restored, notably a fifteenth-century pietà.

TRADITIONAL MARKETS

Customs and traditions tend to survive particularly well in mountain regions. This also applies to two historical markets that have been held in the town since the Middle Ages. On market day, Glurns is spruced up. Every August 24, the Bartholomew market takes place in the town square and offers a spread of local food. The "Sealamorkt," in contrast, is a fair held on November 2 each year, on All Souls' Day. The name literally translates as "souls' market."

Walking around Glurns, you will notice that all of the old buildings have been restored. No matter whether you are looking at a stately home or an inn, everything looks neat and proper. It is not surprising then that Glurns is often compared to the Bavarian town of Rothenburg, known for its intact medieval architecture. The fact that you will stumble upon fountains and wells, mostly located on corners and crossroads, also has a reason. Up until the 1980s, just 900 inhabitants shared their hometown with many cows, and it was not uncommon for farmers to keep their cattle inside the town walls. In the morning, the cows would be taken out to pasture, and they would be brought back into the city in the evening.

Probably the most famous son of Glurns was an illustrator, Paul Flora, who was born there in 1922. The Austrian caricaturist, illustrator, writer, and graphic designer—who died in Innsbruck in 2009 but is buried in the St. Pankratius cemetery—gained international fame. Many of his drawings depict Glurns scenes.

LIVE AND BE MERRY

In Glurns, you can easily spend the night right in the town center and enjoy all its amenities—for example, in the historical Hotel Grüner Baum. A guesthouse with a restaurant was established on this site as early as 1730. Smartly modernized since then, the hotel now offers all modern conveniences. The on-site restaurant serves local delicacies as well as wine grown in the region. The parlor dates back to the early nineteenth century. History also awaits in Café Schöpf, which serves Austrian-inspired cakes. In fair weather, consider renting a bike and cycling through one of the town gates into the countryside—for example, to Mals (Malles Venosta in Italian), another picturesque village less than a twenty-minute bike ride away. Mals is at an altitude of almost 3,280 feet (1,000 meters) and is considered to be one of the sunniest places in South Tyrol.

LEARN MORE
Glurns: www.glurns.eu

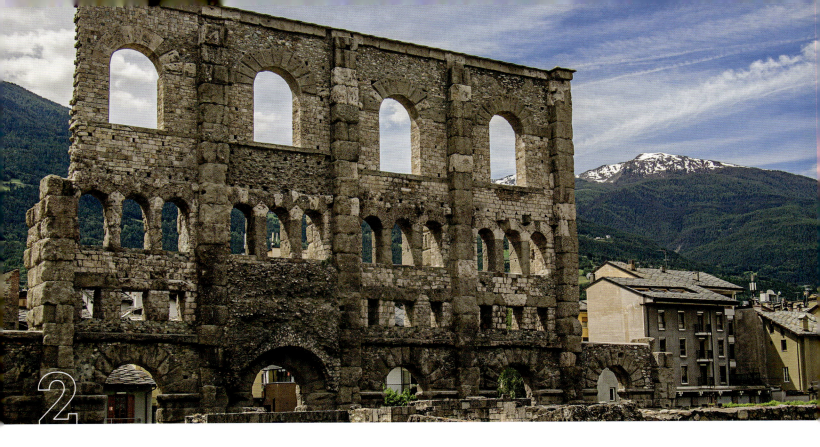

AOSTA – THE WILD AND ROMANTIC MOUNTAIN RESORT

A LONG HISTORY IN BIG SCENERY

Surrounded by breathtaking Alpine peaks, this small town is more than just the ideal starting point for summer hikes and ski tours in the winter. Visitors will encounter cultural monuments dating back around 2,000 years here in Italy's far north.

Who would want to drive all the way to Aosta? Is there anything special to see there? This is a common retort, even from Italians. Unless you are a keen skier or mountaineer, you probably would not have made the trek to the autonomous region of Aosta Valley, including its small capital at an altitude of around 2,000 feet (600 meters). It is home to almost 35,000 inhabitants.

ROMAN TOWN IN THE MOUNTAINS

However, giving Aosta a miss means truly missing out. Surrounded by gigantic mountains, such as Monte Emilius at a height of more than 11,677 feet (3,559 meters), Gran Paradiso at 13,323 feet (4,061 meters), and Mont Dolent at 12,543 feet (3,823 meters), Aosta, which was founded as a garrison town by Julius Caesar in 25 BCE, has much to offer—even without hiking gear or ski boots in tow.

Much remains from the glorious Roman period, such as the 36-foot-tall (11 meters) Arco di Augusto. The antique Arch of Augustus, one of the first buildings erected in the town, can easily compete with others found throughout Italy. The reason why this triumphal arch has been so well preserved to this day is probably that, in the early Middle Ages, a so-called Saint-Voût—an image of Jesus Christ—was mounted on the inside of the arch and later replaced with an iron crucifix. The rather squat monument also served as a habitation in the fourteenth century: in 1318, a local noble family converted the arch into a fortification. Also worth admiring are the impressive ruins of the former Teatro Romano, which stand at a height of

OPPOSITE: **THE ROMANS ALSO LEFT THEIR MARK ON AOSTA, IN THE FAR NORTHWEST OF ITALY.** *LEFT:* **EVEN AN ALMOST INTACT ROMAN TRIUMPHAL ARCH HAS STOOD THE TEST OF TIME.**

72 feet (22 meters). The Porta Praetoria, an ancient city gate, was part of the Roman town wall and was built from large stone blocks.

WITNESSES OF TURBULENT TIMES

Aosta's heyday was in the Middle Ages. Strategically located between France and Italy, the town developed into an important trade center and a hub for goods of all kinds.

The Romanesque church built in the tenth century is worth a visit. Collegiata dei Santi Pietro e Orso (the Collegiate Church of Saint Ursus) is still dominated today by an impressive "campanile," a typical Italian free-standing bell tower. This house of worship was renovated and altered in the following centuries, and it now features a Gothic interior, Romanesque frescoes, and magnificent carved wooden choir stalls from the fifteenth century. A staircase leads down to the ancient crypt with its vaulted ceiling. The church treasury proves just how rich the citizens of Aosta were in the Middle Ages.

Aosta Cathedral is another product of the Middle Ages featuring a Gothic interior, although the beautiful façade stems from the baroque period. Rare hand-painted stained glass windows from the fourteenth century have witnessed the turmoil of the ages.

Romans built for eternity, and so, even after the fall of the Roman Empire, the city wall was used as a defensive structure for centuries to come. Choose a sunny day to explore it—especially the western part, which has been particularly well preserved. In total, it encloses a rectangle of about 2,400 by 1,900 feet (720 by 580 meters).

If the summer heat gets to you in Aosta, we recommend a trip to the Roman Cryptoporticus, an underground vault that is always cool—although experts still puzzle over its intended use.

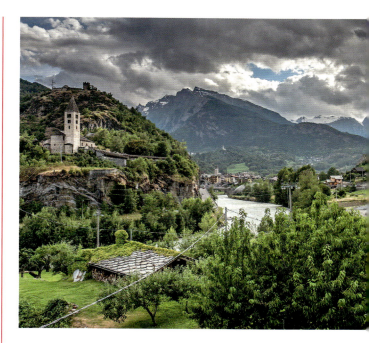

GRESSAN – A DREAM OF A VILLAGE

Less than a ten-minute drive from Aosta lies the pretty Roman-built village of Gressan in a dramatic mountain setting, surrounded by orchards. All of the village churches and chapels date back to the Middle Ages. The campanile of the Chiesa della Madeleine is one of the most beautiful in the entire Aosta Valley. Stop to try the local delicacies in the restaurants of Gressan, Aosta, and the surrounding area. These include fondue, "polenta concia" (cornmeal with sharp Toma cheese), and also the hearty "seupa à la Vapelenentse," a cheese soup with butter, bread, and cinnamon. These go very well with one of the aromatic local wines produced in the valley. L'Uva e Un Quarto, a wine bar in Aosta at Via Challand 21/A, serves only the best wines.

LEARN MORE
Aosta Valley: www.lovevda.it
Gressan: www.comune.gressan.ao.it

ORTA SAN GIULIO – HIDDEN IN THE MOUNTAINS
PICTURESQUE IDYLL

A romantic mountain lake and an enchanted island: while San Giulio Island and Lake Orta do not feature on many tourist maps, they are certainly worth a day trip to the north of the region of Piedmont.

This glacial lake is not very big; at a little under 8 square miles (20 square kilometers), it measures just under 2 by 8 miles (3 by 13 kilometers) and is only 470 feet (143 meters) deep. Lake Orta lies at an altitude of about 980 feet (300 meters) and is flanked by mountains on three sides. Their forest-covered slopes are home to horse chestnut, fir, spruce, and beech trees, which form a dense canopy that is only rarely disrupted by buildings. Here, you get to see Italy as if in a Romantic painting from the nineteenth century.

Access to the lake itself is through the town of Orta San Giulio, located right by the water. With a population of just 1,300, it is considered one of the most beautiful municipalities in Italy. All its historical buildings look spick-and-span. Its promenade has many cafés and bars and is worth a leisurely stroll. The Palazzo della Comunità, the old town hall with its open portico, dates back to the late sixteenth century. Make sure to visit "La Motta," the parish church dating from 1485.

AN ENCHANTED ISLAND

A trip on one of the traditional wooden boats from Orta San Giulio to San Giulio Island is an experience you do not want to miss. It is only a stone's throw from the shore (about 1,300 feet or 400 meters), and yet you enter another world—especially in bad weather. The town by the lake is generally quiet and void of any hubbub. But the peace and tranquility on this completely built-up island immediately cast a spell on its visitors. The island's name derives from an ancient Greek hero, who is

said to have freed the isle—which is the only one in the lake and is about 900 by 460 feet (275 by 140 meters) in size—from the claws of a dragon. What is certain, however, is that San Giulio has been inhabited since the Stone Age. Then came the Romans, followed by the first Christian church in the fourth century.

THE BASILICA GREETS FROM AFAR

San Giulio Island is dominated by its eponymous basilica. Pious tradition maintains that a certain Giulio from Greece evangelized the island and built its first chapel. In the Middle Ages, the isle was fortified by Lombardic rulers, who built the basilica in the twelfth century on the remains of an early Christian church dating from the fifth century.

The basilica features a plain Romanesque façade with two slender spires. The interior, with its nave and two nave aisles, still passes as essentially Romanesque, even though later, in the Renaissance and baroque eras, the church was decorated with murals. Beautiful to look at is a pulpit from the twelfth century, which is most certainly among the best preserved in Northern Italy. Besides the traditional four evangelists, it is embellished with pagan centaurs and mythical creatures typical of medieval art. The earthly remains of Saint Giulio are kept in a richly decorated baroque reliquary.

TRAFFIC-FREE ALLEYS

After a visit to the basilica, take a stroll through the picturesque alleys of the island village, with its town palaces, historical residential buildings, and welcoming restaurants. Particularly appealing is an aperitif, followed by dinner with a view to the opposite shore as the fading natural daylight gives way to artificial light.

In the summer, the island gets its musical groove on. During an annual festival, classical concerts take place every evening. The beauty of San Giulio Island has inspired many writers and movie-makers, including Umberto Eco and director Giuseppe Tornatore.

OPPOSITE: **FROM THE LAKESIDE, YOU CAN TAKE IN THE VIEW OVER TO SAN GIULIO ISLAND—A PLEASURE AT ANY TIME OF THE DAY AND IN ANY WEATHER.** ABOVE: **THE PAINTED DOME OF THE ISLAND BASILICA IS REGARDED AS A TRIUMPH OF BAROQUE ART.**

THE HOLY MOUNTAIN

In the vicinity of Orta San Giulio is a so-called "Sacro Monte," a holy mountain. The religious complex consists of twenty chapels dedicated to the life of Francis of Assisi. The painted chapels were created between 1591 and the early seventeenth century. It is a tradition to walk from one chapel to the next in prayer—a romantic religious stroll amidst nature at an altitude of around 1,300 feet (400 meters). The paintings were created by local artists and have been very well preserved. The custom of these holy mountains is exclusive to the northwest of Italy, and only a few of these chapel hills remain as intact as the Sacro Monte near Orta San Giulio.

LEARN MORE
Sacro Monte: www.sacrimonti.org

COMO – THE SMALL TOWN BY A PICTURESQUE LAKESIDE

EMBRACED BY THE LAKE

Local and foreign movie stars, politicians, and entrepreneurs know only too well why they choose to spend time in Como and to buy gorgeous mansions by the lake. Quality of life is a priority here—in a setting that is simply picture-perfect.

Even when it rains in Como, the old town looks simply enticing. This may be because it rarely gets crowded here, and visitors can enjoy the romantic side of the historical town center in complete tranquility—taking in spots such as the Piazza del Duomo, which is surrounded by elegant buildings from different eras, and the medieval Palazzo Broletto, where the town hall is located. Built in the thirteenth century and renovated in the sixteenth century, the building is completed by its tower from 1927.

The cathedral is rightly regarded as the most impressive building in Como, a town that is home to 85,000 residents. The cathedral is both the religious and the urban heart of the city and one of the most beautiful sacred buildings in all of Lombardy. Both Italian and northern European influences come together here, much like everywhere else in Northern Italy. The cathedral's construction began in the fourteenth century. The star of baroque architecture, Filippo Juvarra of Turin, completed the cathedral in 1723 and crowned it with a baroque dome. Also interesting are the huge precious tapestries from the sixteenth century that are suspended from the high-ceilinged interior.

WALKS OF DISCOVERY

With its small squares, its old palaces, and a few charming museums, Como is made for strolling. Exuding medieval charm are many of the churches, such as Sant'Abbondio from the eleventh century. Its interior has four nave aisles, divided from the central nave by a forest of columns, and features rare murals from the fourteenth century. Examples of characteristic Lombard paintings from the seventeenth and

OPPOSITE: **A GEM RIGHT BY THE LAKE: COMO OFFERS ART, ARCHITECTURE, AND ENTICING WALKS ALONG THE SHORE.**
LEFT: **BAUHAUS AND FASCISM: IN COMO THESE TWO (ARTISTIC) MOVEMENTS FORM AN UNUSUAL SYMBIOSIS.**

eighteenth centuries can be found in the Pinacoteca Civica. These also tell the story of the region's former wealth. The silk trade brought the city of Como prosperity. The history of silk production and all the precious things that were made of the silkworms' threads can be explored at the Museo della Seta.

A building unique in all of Italy was erected in the city center, at the Piazza del Popolo. The so-called Casa del Fascio was constructed between 1932 and 1936. Its architect, Giuseppe Terragni, designed this former Como headquarters of the Italian Fascist Party. In contrast to the Third Reich, Benito Mussolini's Italy appreciated the rationalist style of Bauhaus architecture. The Casa del Fascio is an elegant building with clean, straight lines; the façade is a dialogue between white solid surfaces and shaded recesses—a masterpiece of early twentieth-century modern architecture!

A LAKE WITHIN THE TOWN

The lakefront is an important part of Como's cityscape. The locals call the 0.6-mile-long (1 kilometer) promenade "Lungolario." It hugs the winding shore and hosts cafés, such as Terminus with its Art Nouveau interiors, or the bar of the Hotel Metropole Suisse—two perfect places for an early evening aperitif. This is also where the pleasure boats take off across the narrow but 28-mile-long (46 kilometers) lake.

In the nineteenth century, wealthy citizens built luxury mansions on the lake's banks, such as the Villa Geno or the palace housing the Fondazione Ratti, home to the textile museum. Villa Olmo, however, which is perhaps the most elegant of them all, dates back to the 1780s. Napoleon and Joseph Radetzky, Prince Klemens von Metternich, and Ferdinand I of Austria resided here. The park, landscaped in classic Italian style, invites visitors to take a walk.

THE BALCONY OF LAKE COMO

Brunate is a kind of viewing platform: from up here, about 1,640 feet (500 meters) above the city, visitors can enjoy what is likely the most beautiful view of Lake Como and the surrounding mountains of the Southern Alps. The most convenient way to reach the town of Brunate is by taking the funicular that was built over one hundred years ago. The journey only takes a few minutes. Up here, in these lofty heights, small hotels, romantic restaurants, and cafés offer ideal places to relax. But be mindful: only make the journey in good weather and preferably in time for sunset.

LEARN MORE
Como: www.visitcomo.eu/en
Cathedral: www.cattedraledicomo.it/en

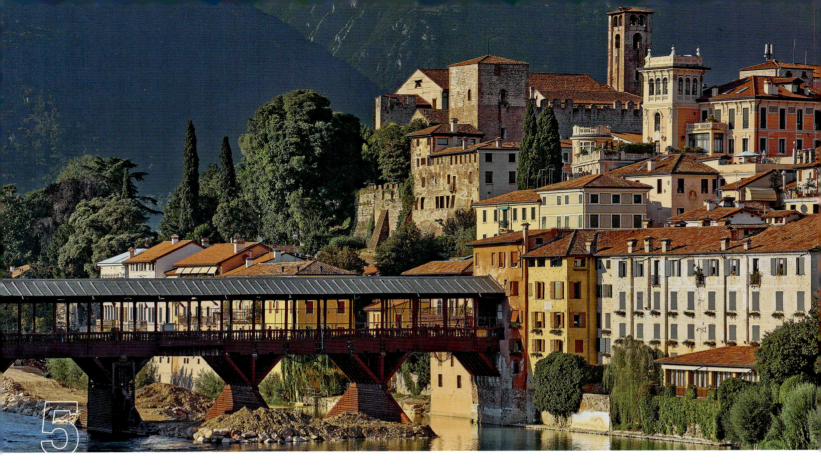

5

BASSANO DEL GRAPPA – THE HIGH-PROOF DELIGHT

CHEERS TO BASSANO!

This small town is not only charming and features one of the most famous bridges in Italy, but it also distills a world-famous drink. Strolling and tasting a glass of grappa go together very nicely in Bassano.

Woe betide visitors to Bassano del Grappa who dare to mention that grappa, a type of pomace brandy, is also distilled in the Italian part of Switzerland! For the around 38,000 inhabitants of this small town situated in a picturesque area of the Vicenza province, this alcoholic drink with a proof of 70 to 120 clearly belongs to Bassano alone. Anyone who claims otherwise is a "bugiardo" (liar).

Grappa, as any bartender in Bassano would tell you, is distilled from the fermented leftovers—the pomace—of winemaking. The best types of grappa are made from red grapes. The brownish tint comes from the aging process in wooden barrels. The type of barrel wood also determines the drink's aroma and flavor. The best way to taste the various products is by visiting one of the pleasant wine bars of Bassano—ideally in the evening after a walk through the town.

There are many things to marvel at in the Museo Civico, which also hosts the Pinacoteca. It begs to be visited with a clear head—that is, prior to any grappa delectation. The museum is housed in a former convent, the Convento dei Minori. The permanent collection of paintings includes several masterpieces one might not have expected here, such as work by Jacopo Bassano, a Renaissance painter who was born in 1510 in—you guessed it—Bassano and who also died in the town in 1592. You can also marvel at works by the Venetian painters Giovanni Battista Tiepolo and Pietro Longhi. A curious selection of exhibits is the collection of memorabilia that Tito Gobbi bequeathed to the museum. Gobbi was also a Bassano local and one of Italy's most famous baritones. He died in Rome in 1984.

DESIGNED FOR CENTURIES

Bassano's most famous building is a bridge. In 1569, Andrea Palladio planned the Ponte Vecchio, the old bridge, in line with the previous passage across the river, which had been washed away by a flood. Palladio is considered one of Italy's most famous Renaissance architects. The so-called Palladian villas in the northeast of Italy bear his characteristic elegant and classic mark, modeled on Roman antiquity. His bridge construction lasted for over two hundred years—until it was damaged by yet another flood. Several destructions followed, and the bridge was even immortalized in a soldiers' song. To this day, every reconstruction is based on Palladio's design with its four slender bays, which hardly interrupt the flow of the Brenta River.

On a walk through the lovingly restored old town, visitors will come across many historical buildings, medieval palaces, and Renaissance houses, as well as baroque churches. There are not many tourists here—and the few you'll meet will gather around the bridge. You will find all the tourist sites in direct vicinity to the Piazza della Libertà, just a stone's throw away from the Ponte Vecchio: the museum, the churches of San Francesco and San Giovanni Battista, and the Palazzo del Municipio from the thirteenth century.

OPPOSITE: **JUST LIKE A PICTURESQUE STAGE SET: THE OLD TOWN OF BASSANO WITH THE PONTE VECCHIO BRIDGE.**
BELOW: **GRAPPA TASTINGS ARE POSSIBLE AND POPULAR IN EVERY BAR IN TOWN.**

And if you don't fancy trying a locally distilled grappa after your tour, you only have yourself to blame. Rumor has it that in Bassano, even toddlers get to suck on a finger dipped in grappa, so local children develop a taste for grappa from an early age.

MODERN GRAPPA BUBBLES

The historical distillery Nardini was founded in the late 1770s. To celebrate its 225th anniversary in 2004, the company commissioned the Roman architect Massimiliano Fuksas to design a new building to represent the local distillates in a modern way. Fuksas built them a beetle-shaped building consisting of accessible glass and steel bubbles. Inside this most modern of Bassano sites are a conference room, a research center (for grappa, of course), and tasting rooms. Be tempted to taste one of Nardini's own grappas inside the green glass bubbles, especially the aged ones.

LEARN MORE
Bassano del Grappa: www.veneto.eu
Nardini: www.nardini.it

AQUILEIA – THE MIGHTY BISHOP'S SEE
BASILICA OF SUPERLATIVES

In Aquileia's long and eventful history, most of the town's historical buildings got lost. But one church has survived all destruction. It is so richly decorated that any detour to the small town with only 3,200 inhabitants is worth your while.

There are not many sites in Aquileia in the Friuli-Venezia Giulia region; as early as the third century, the Romans in this northeastern corner of the Italian boot had to contend with invading Barbarian tribes. Battles and destruction abounded—but the basilica withstood it all. A lucky escape!

GERMAN-STYLE CHURCH
The design of the Romanesque basilica from the early eleventh century was based on similar churches in what is now Lower Saxony, Germany—first and foremost on St. Michael's Church in Hildesheim, which was completed just a little while earlier. Like its German role model, the Basilica di Santa Maria Assunta is a fairly large church, measuring 75 feet (23 meters) high, 98 feet (30 meters) wide, and almost 217 feet (66 meters) long.

The most precious part of this basilica is its interior design. The floor mosaics are among the most beautiful, the most abundant in terms of motifs, and the best preserved in Europe. They were created over various centuries and are therefore stacked on top of each other. A large part of these mosaics dates back to the fourth century, while other parts are more recent. Unsurprisingly, the floor is quite uneven, but visitors can explore it from glass walkways. A total of 8,180 square feet (760 square meters) are covered with small and minuscule mosaic tiles. It's a record-breaking work of art: it features one of

OPPOSITE: **BUILT FROM THE MAGNIFICENT REMAINS OF ANTIQUITY AND ADORNED WITH A PAGAN FLOOR MOSAIC: THE BASILICA OF AQUILEIA.** LEFT: **THE ENTIRE SURROUNDINGS ARE PART OF AN ARCHAEOLOGICAL EXCAVATION SITE.**

the oldest and largest Christian mosaics in the Western world.

Some of these mosaics depict portraits; for example, one features of one of the church donors. According to experts, Emperor Constantine, the first Christian emperor, is portrayed here as well, as is his mother Helena, who was said to have come from a humble background and who was later canonized by the Catholic Church. Emperor Constantine is said to have visited Aquileia between 313 and 333 CE. Being in the emperor's favor, the city was endowed with great financial support and prospered. Many representative buildings were erected, such as the Roman circus and the amphitheater. The remains of these structures from late antiquity can be viewed in the immediate vicinity of the basilica. Surrounded by lush nature, this archaeological site is a rather romantic spot.

PATRONS AND EMPERORS

Many corners of the mosaic floor give the impression of a mega comic strip. For example, there is the story of Jonah, who is swallowed up by a sea monster and then spit out again. Or Jonah, yet again, resting under a pergola, or praying to God. There's also a colorful carpet to be marveled at for hours on end. These late antique images feature realistic representations, limiting the design elements to the essentials—and thus creating a simple visual language that is easily understood by everyone.

Also common are allegories with Christian symbolism: fish, grapes, and birds. Interestingly, these floors resemble those of the Bardo National Museum in Tunis, Tunisia. It is thought that the Aquileia mosaics were created by the same artists who embellished the mansions of rich landowners in the North African provinces.

Likewise, the eighty-three bishops ruling over Aquileia from late antiquity to the eighteenth century were wealthy and powerful. Thanks to its advantageous transport links, many merchants and tradespeople passed through the town.

The Patriarchate of Aquileia was eventually suppressed in 1751. From then on, the city ceased to be a seat of bishops, and the diocese was relegated to a so-called titular see.

CREATURE COMFORTS

After a visit to the basilica, it is time for temptation. The Pasticceria Mosaico lures gourmets in with wine-flavored ice cream made with Malvasia, Savagnin, and Refosco grape juice. In the restaurant of the Hotel Patriarchi, the gnocchi with smoked ricotta cheese is to be recommended. A local specialty bread is "gubana," a puff pastry or bread dough strudel with candied fruit, chocolate, nuts, sultanas, and sweet wine. La Colombara serves pickled sardines with prosecco and marinated zucchini. It goes without saying that Aquileia's bars serve local wines from the Friuli region. This wine region is not as well known outside Italy, but it nevertheless produces excellent drinks, especially exquisite white wines such as Aquileia Refosco or Carso.

LEARN MORE
Aquileia: www.turismofvg.it
Pasticceria Mosaico: www.pasticceriamosaico.com

BRESCIA – A WORLD HERITAGE TOWN IN A PRIME LOCATION
A GEM OF AN OLD TOWN

Founded by the Romans, this settlement had grown into an important commercial center by the Middle Ages. The many magnificent buildings in the almost intact old town bear witness to the wealth of its citizens. The fact that Lake Garda and Milan are close by only enhances Brescia's appeal.

Brescia's town center is an urban paradise made for a stroll—though, inexplicably, it is rarely a point of call for foreign tourists. The center of this city, with its almost 200,000 inhabitants, is marked by the Piazza della Loggia, a square almost entirely lined with historical buildings in the Venetian style. The elegant loggia dates back to the Renaissance. Renaissance architect Andrea Palladio is said to have contributed to its harmonious design.

STRANGE NEIGHBORS

Brescia's most magnificent medieval building is undoubtedly "La Rotonda" from the eleventh century. This circular former cathedral, reminiscent of an ancient assembly hall, is located right next to the new cathedral dating from the seventeenth century—two curious neighbors. Opposite the cathedrals is the Palazzo Broletto. The palace is one of the most impressive secular buildings in the city, built in the twelfth century. The municipal government chose Broletto as its seat in the Middle Ages when the first politically independent municipalities were set up in Northern Italy. It features a tower known as the city tower or "Tower of the People," which underlines the Broletto's importance.

The Pinacoteca Tosio Martinengo is proof that Brescia has a long-standing artistic tradition. This collection of paintings is on a par with larger ones in Milan or elsewhere. The exhibition rooms are full of masterpieces from the breadth of Italian art history, ranging from Lorenzo Lotto and Jacopo

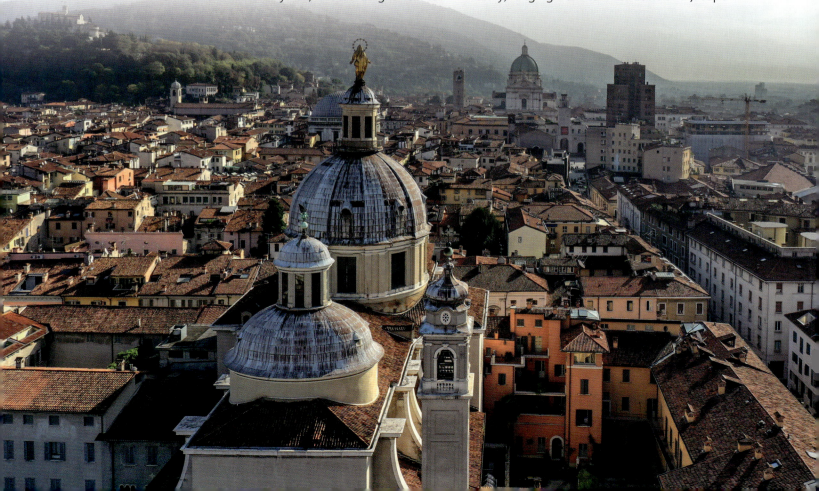

OPPOSITE: **INEXPLICABLY IGNORED BY FOREIGN VISITORS: THE CHARMING OLD TOWN OF BRESCIA.** LEFT: **THE PIAZZA DELLA LOGGIA WITH A MAGNIFICENT BUILDING BY RENAISSANCE STAR PALLADIO CONSTITUTES THE CENTER OF THE OLD TOWN.**

Tintoretto to Vincenzo Foppa and many more, mostly Lombard painters.

Among the numerous old churches, two stand out in particular: the Basilica San Salvatore from the High Middle Ages rises from the remains of the formerly wealthy Roman city. The frescoes inside date to the eighth to the fifteenth centuries. Santi Nazaro e Celso, on the other hand, has a baroque façade and inside features one of Titian's masterworks, the *Averoldi Polyptych*, dating from 1522. Other Renaissance and baroque paintings in this church are also worth a second look.

TREASURES FROM BRIXIA

Right in the middle of the old town is the imposing ancient Roman forum with the assembly square and the impressive remains of the Temple of the Capitoline Triad from the first century. The extensive grounds also house the Museo Romano, which has very charming finds on display from the ancient city that used to bear the Latin name Brixia. The complex of ancient ruins also includes an amphitheater from the third century. The theater was in use until the Middle Ages; it was here that public meetings of free citizens took place. The Roman theater is of high architectural value since it survived—almost unscathed—a severe earthquake shaking Brescia in the fifth century. It could accommodate up to 15,000 people.

The Santa Giulia Museum is located on the ancient road axis Decumanus Maximus. Today, the "city museum" is housed in an extraordinarily well-preserved monastery from the Langobardic period. On approximately 150,000 square feet (14,000 square meters) of exhibition space, it displays archaeological and artistic finds from almost two thousand years of the city's history, including a very rare splendid crucifix from the time of the Carolingians, Renaissance frescoes, ancient mosaic floors, and murals.

ANCIENT ANGEL

In 1826, archaeological excavation works in the Capitolium in the heart of Brescia prised a unique sculpture from the earth. Today, it is presented to the visitors at the place where it was found. The piece is a 77-inch (195 centimeters) bronze work depicting a young woman with two large wings on her back. The sculpture probably dates back to 250 BCE. It was gifted to the ancient city of Brixia by Emperor Augustus as a symbol of promoting the municipality to the status of a city, a Colonia Augusta. The fact that the bronze survived the rigors of Barbaric invaders at the end of the Roman Empire unscathed is thanks to some unknown people who hid it in a hollow space near the Capitol.

LEARN MORE
Tourist Office: www.bresciatourism.it/en/
Santa Giulia Museum: www.bresciamusei.com/en/

TREVISO – MAINLAND VENICE IN MINIATURE

CLOSE TO THE WATER'S EDGE

Palaces, small canals, medieval flair, and plenty of tranquility: Treviso is one of those typical Italian towns that has a lot to offer but has somehow been ignored by the tourist hype. Lucky for those who do decide to explore the Veneto region!

The small town is entirely surrounded by water, although the home to 80,000 residents is located on the mainland, and there is no lake in sight. Treviso's special feature is the Sile River and the various waterways it feeds. The city center, which forms an almost perfect rectangle, is surrounded on three sides by canals. The fourth border is the river itself. A fluid wall, if you like, is the gateway to an intact city center.

Treviso offers a lot to discover. The Gothic church of San Nicolò, built in the thirteenth and fourteenth centuries, features one nave and two aisles, five chapels, and huge pilasters supporting the roof, and it is a masterpiece of northeastern Italian architecture. The abundance of art includes frescoes by Tommaso da Modena, paintings by the Lombard School, and a historical and fully functioning organ. The altarpiece *Madonna and Child with Six Saints* from the early sixteenth century and the magnificent funeral monument to the Venetian senator Agostino Onigo alone are worth the visit.

NORTHERN EUROPEAN INFLUENCES

This and other churches clearly show how Italian and Northern European influences combine here and everywhere else in Treviso. Many of the Gothic elements recall similar designs popular north of the Alps. These traits are mainly owed to close trade relations between the citizens of Treviso and business people north of the Alps. As far back as the early Middle Ages, local residents entertained business relations both with

OPPOSITE: **IMPRESSIVE ARCHITECTURE: TREVISO IS VENICE IN MINIATURE WITHOUT MASS TOURISM, BUT WITH A LOT OF LOCAL COLOR.** *LEFT*: **JUST LIKE IN VENICE, MAN-MADE CANALS INTERSPERSE THE TOWN AND OFFER REFLECTIVE SURFACES FOR THE NUMEROUS PALAZZI.**

merchants in Southern Italy and the German Empire. The Museo Civico Luigi Bailo exhibits a display of important paintings. It includes works by Giovanni Bellini and Cima da Conegliano, Lorenzo Lotto, Titian, and many others.

A stop at the cathedral is, of course, a must for any visitor. Erected in the Middle Ages, it was renovated and converted several times; it now houses a kind of art museum. Works by important painters—including Titian—are displayed on altars and in chapels. The baptistery, a Romanesque chapel linked to the cathedral, is decorated with frescoes and ancient reliefs.

Starting at the square outside the cathedral, a city stroll takes you past rustic trattorias and delicatessens selling local specialties, eventually arriving at the Piazza dei Signori. Important secular buildings from the late Middle Ages and the early Renaissance line the main civic square in Treviso. A beautiful example is the Loggia dei Cavalieri from the thirteenth century, where local nobility used to meet to decide on politics.

ALONG THE WATERWAYS

Narrow waterways lead through the old town, not unlike the canals in Venice. They are called "buranelli." The name derives from the inhabitants of the island of Burano in the Venetian Lagoon. They owned houses in Treviso to provide the small town, located about 25 miles (40 kilometers) inland, with fresh fish. Just like in Venice, the canals used to be trade routes for goods of all kinds. Along some of these waterways are old houses over archways designed to shield tradespeople and buyers from the rain. Depending on the weather, the canals develop a unique and special atmosphere. At nightfall, they are illuminated in a scenographic way.

If you let yourself be carried away in this maze of alleyways in the old town, you quickly lose your sense of orientation—an extremely charming experience. On your tour, you will come across an island in the middle of a canal called Pescheria. This is one of Treviso's most magical places: at this place, where people have sold fish for centuries, many of the alleys and canals converge.

FAMOUS VEGETABLE

Radicchio Rosso di Treviso is a local specialty in red and white: a crisp vegetable with an unforgettable subtly bitter taste. Although Treviso doesn't have the monopoly on its production (neighboring municipalities grow the vegetable as well), experts say the best radicchio comes from the city of canals. A typical winter vegetable, it is used in salads, as a pasta filling, and in almost all other dishes. There is even a locally brewed Treviso beer flavored with radicchio. A local specialty tea also shares this taste profile. A consortium ensures that all available radicchio really only comes from Treviso and its surrounding area. Of course, the delicacy boasts the coveted IGP label, the registered "protected geographical indication" seal certifying its origin and quality.

LEARN MORE
Treviso: www.visittreviso.it

TORCELLO – THE DREAMY ISLAND
REFUGE IN THE LAGOON

Among the many islands off the coast of Venice, there is one that has a special kind of appeal and yet has been spared by mass tourism. But a brief stopover would not do Torcello justice; it is only if you grant it a little time that the island reveals all its charms.

Ernest Hemingway loved Torcello. He went hunting here and stayed in the Locanda Cipriani, which used to be the country house of the owners of Harry's Bar in Venice. Whether the renowned American writer deepened his close friendship with the beautiful countess Adriana Ivancich on the island of Torcello—in his hotel room or in his small house Casarossa—remains unclear. What is clear, however, is that the author fell in love with the island.

A PLACE OF REFUGE FOR 1,500 YEARS

What is also certain is that Torcello, at the very edge of the Roman Empire, was one of the first islands in the lagoon where people from the mainland settled to be safe from possible attacks by the Barbarians. These people supposedly called themselves "Turris." They named the island "Turricellum," which later became Torcello.

Since 638 CE, the island has been a diocese. Clergymen brought important relics with them and maintained good relations with merchants. Between the sixth and the ninth centuries, Torcello developed into an important commercial center. Around 20,000 people are said to have lived here at one time—on only 0.17 square miles (0.44 square kilometers) of land! Today, there are just under twenty people left on Torcello, surrounded by nature, peace, and astonishing art.

PRECIOUS SACRED ART

There are two churches to visit, with Santa Maria Assunta being one of the most important churches as far as the art history of the whole of northeastern Italy is concerned. Built in the seventh century, expanded in the eleventh century, and again in the fifteenth century, the house of worship now appears in the Romanesque style. Ancient and Byzantine columns split the nave and two aisles and support the ceiling. The mosaic floor is a masterpiece from the eleventh century. The entire interior west wall is decorated with a gold background mosaic from the twelfth and thirteenth centuries. The intact work of art depicts the Last Judgment in partly graphic detail. Throughout the church, there are mosaics in the Byzantine style. Especially beautiful is one in the apse, which shows the Madonna with the infant Jesus. At the entrance portal in the lunette is another magnificent golden mosaic of the Blessed Mother. Looking closely at the altar, you will discover an inscription with the date "639" on the left. This indicates the year in which the church was founded—and is the oldest historical document in Venetian history.

The church of Santa Fosca, on the other hand, built above the relics of the eponymous martyr, is quite plain on the inside. Yet the Romanesque building dating from the eleventh century exudes great tranquility, as if it was made for meditation.

HIKING AND RELAXING

Torcello is the ideal place to relax after the hustle and bustle of Venice. Inviting walking trails suggest a hike, and the only island hotel is perfect for a break; it is not particularly cheap, but very enchanting. Although it looks like a simple hostel, the hotel, which has been in existence since 1934, offers five guest rooms with all modern conveniences. It also boasts a restaurant that is one of the best in the lagoon. Besides Hemingway, the Locanda hosted and catered for several illustrious guests, such as Prince Charles and Lady Diana, Elton John, and other celebrities. It isn't for everyone, but if you are after a very special experience for a few days, on an island in the middle of the lagoon, you will find it here.

OPPOSITE: **AWAY FROM THE VENETIAN HYPE: THE REMOTE LAGOON ISLAND OF TORCELLO WITH ITS FAMOUS CHURCH.** *ABOVE*: **RECENT RESEARCH REVEALED THAT THE CHURCH AND ITS MURALS WERE CREATED UNDER THE INFLUENCE OF THE CAROLINGIANS.**

COZY CROSSING

Torcello is easily reached by water taxi, since the island is not far from St. Mark's Square. But you should take your time to get to it. The vaporetto waterbus, which is also considerably cheaper than the expensive water taxi, takes a little over an hour. It stops at various other islands, allowing you to get a glimpse of them on the way. This leisurely one-hour ride through the lagoon creates a distance from the hectic city center and allows you to find inner calm. If you travel to Torcello this way, you are already in the right mood to enter the island's slow way of life.

LEARN MORE
Torcello: www.turismovenezia.it
Locanda Cipriani: www.locandacipriani.com
ACTV, waterbuses: www.muoversi.venezia.it

THIS PAGE: **THE PIAZZA SAN CARLO IS THE BAROQUE BEATING HEART OF THE FORMER ROYAL CITY OF TURIN.** *OPPOSITE:* **FROM THE HILLTOPS, YOU GET A FANTASTIC VIEW OF TURIN AND THE ALPS—WHICH APPEAR VERY CLOSE IN GOOD WEATHER.**

TURIN – THE COOL CLASSIC

FIAT, BAROQUE SOPHISTICATION, AND A UNIQUE VIBE

The former capital of the Kingdom of Italy brims with baroque palaces, elegant coffee houses, a car racing track on a factory roof, and the most important Egyptian museum outside of Cairo. And the mountains are just around the corner.

Only a few Italian cities have as much to offer as Turin on the one hand, yet have been as neglected by tourists to Italy on the other. This may be due to its geographical location in the northwest of Italy—but, often, tourists bypass Turin because they don't know what they are missing in this city of 890,000 inhabitants.

PROUD BUILDINGS
The Piedmontese royal family wanted to leave a mark with regard to art and architecture that could rival their powerful neighbor, France. And so, in the eighteenth century, a modern city was born, with straight streets and avenues flanked by representative buildings whose style betrays their French inspiration. One of these structures is the Palazzo Madama in the heart of the historical center, a masterpiece by architect Filippo Juvarra, whose elegant and uncluttered baroque style was very much en vogue in Turin in the eighteenth century. The Palazzo Madama now houses the Museo Civico d'Arte Antica, a collection of paintings with major works by artists such as Antonello da Messina and Jan van Eyck.

The Renaissance cathedral was magnificently restored in the baroque era. The Cappella della Sacra Sindone from the late seventeenth century houses the Holy Shroud of Turin, one of the most important and simultaneously most scientifically contested relics of Catholic Christianity.

Scattered across the city center, which saw major changes throughout the nineteenth and twentieth centuries, are several magnificent baroque buildings that bore witness to the construction fever of the kings of Savoy. In recent years, these architectural gems have been painstakingly restored—among them the Royal Armory, a section of the Royal Palace of Turin. It houses one of the world's most plentiful collections of arms and armor. The Piazza San Carlo, Turin's main square, was also elegantly restored; here, eighteenth-century palazzi with archways face each other in a symmetrical composition. Two baroque churches stand like sentinels at the southern end of the square, framing the view as if on a stage.

It was in the Palazzo Carignano, a particularly French-looking baroque-era building, that Italian patriots proclaimed the Kingdom of Italy in 1861. Ten years after the event, the palace's gardens were transformed into the Piazza Carlo Alberto. An equestrian statue commemorates the king, who became more and more open to liberal ideas in the middle of the nineteenth century.

The little Palazzina di Caccia di Stupinigi on the outskirts of the city is particularly attractive. King Vittorio Amedeo II commissioned Filippo Juvarra to build him what might be considered the largest, most beautiful, and most elegant hunting lodge in Italy.

CITY OF MUSEUMS

Italy's fourth largest city boasts a host of unique museums. Besides remarkably rich collections, such as one of the most important art collections in Europe in the Sabauda Gallery, Turin is home to the most important movie museum in the country, the National Museum of Cinema. This interactive museum was fitted into the unusual Mole

LEFT: THE STUPINIGI HUNTING LODGE IS CONSIDERED A CASTLE OF SUPERLATIVES DUE TO ITS SIZE AND SPLENDOR. *ABOVE*: IT LOOKS LIKE A UFO HAS LANDED ON THE ROOF OF THE FORMER FIAT TEST TRACK, WHICH HOUSES A GALLERY FOR TEMPORARY ART EXHIBITIONS.

Antonelliana, a building whose tower, at 549.54 feet (167.5 meters), is visible from far away. The Museo Egizio was completely modernized only a few years ago and scenographically arranged; after the National Museum of Cairo, it is the most important of its kind in the world. On display are Egyptian burial artifacts, works of art, sarcophagi, mummies, and excellently preserved hieroglyphs.

A little outside the historical city center, in the Stabilimento Fiat Lingotto, visitors can admire the Fiat company's test track on the roof of the former factory. Nowadays, the huge building from the 1930s features a minimalist luxury hotel, among other things.

A MECCA FOR CONTEMPORARY ART

And Turin has another ace up its sleeve. The city promotes contemporary art in a way rivaled only by very few other Italian municipalities—both in the private sector, through foundations and galleries, and in the public sector, such as through the Turin Civic Gallery of Modern and Contemporary Art (GAM) and the Museo d'Arte Contemporanea in the Castello di Rivoli just outside the city. Every fall, the city hosts Artissima, one of the most important fairs for contemporary art. A large number of collectors live in the Piedmontese capital and make their art available to the public. One of them is Patrizia Sandretto Re Rebaudengo, who is considered one of the most influential women in the Italian art scene. Fondazione Sandretto Re Rebaudengo is housed in a plain house of art designed by the architect Claudio Silvestrin, and it exhibits the highlights of the influential collector's 1,500-piece collection of international artists. Fondazione Merz presents the works of Mario Merz, who is regarded as one of the most important Italian proponents of the so-called Arte Povera. The museum is located in a former factory.

The GAM is one of the first—and wealthiest—municipal museums of modern and contemporary art in all of Italy. It was founded many years before other municipalities set up similar collections. The GAM exhibits more than 45,000 paintings, photographs, and sculptures, including by many household names of the twentieth century, such as Paul Klee, Michelangelo Pistoletto, and Filippo De Pisis.

The Museo dell'Arte Contemporanea in the Castello di Rivoli—a castle dating back to the tenth century—provides space for contemporary art in all its facets. Time and again, its exhibitions cause real sensations.

HISTORICAL COFFEE HOUSES

Turin is, beside Trieste, Italy's capital of traditional coffee houses. The Belle Epoque café Baratti & Milano, established in 1875, is famous for its "gianduja" chocolate; Café Mulassano, from 1907 and entirely decorated in the Art Nouveau style, is known for inventing the first "tramezzino" sandwiches; and Caffè Confetteria Al Bicerin, which opened in 1793, serves the traditional "bicerin," a popular hot drink made with coffee, chocolate, and milk cream. Caffè Gelateria Fiorio has been serving ice cream creations since 1780; its gianduja ice cream is particularly tasty. The historic Caffè San Carlo, located at the square of the same name, sports a very luxurious interior, decorated with crystal chandeliers, stucco, and plenty of marble. It serves irresistible cakes and gateaus in this impressive setting. Caffè Platti, Caffè Torino, and others shine to this day in the magnificent splendor of the nineteenth century and are still frequented and loved by the locals.

LEARN MORE
Turin: www.turismotorino.org
Museo Egizio: www.museoegizio.it
The Royal Residences: www.residenzereali.it

11

PAVIA – SPIRITUAL GREATNESS AND SIMPLE BEAUTY

THE PEARL OF LOMBARDY

A place where education has been high on the list of priorities since the ninth century, where you will find one of the most impressive Carthusian monasteries of Europe, and where you can enjoy the romantic charm of a small Italian town without the tourist hubbub—Pavia has it all.

As early as 825, Emperor Lothair I, king of Italy and later emperor of the Carolingians, established the so-called Scuola Palatina in this small town founded by the Romans. It was one of the first European educational institutions of the Middle Ages and continued an ancient tradition. Emperor Charles IV founded the University of Pavia in 1361, which quickly grew into one of the most important and influential universities in Italy. Around 1770, Giuseppe Piermarini, the architect of the Milan opera house Teatro alla Scala, created a magnificent new building with a venerable library in the Salone Teresiano commissioned by Habsburg Empress Maria Theresa. The University of Pavia is a testament to the great cultural wealth of this provincial town, which has always been overshadowed by the urban metropolis Milan in the north.

CITY OF TOWERS

The medieval poets Petrarca and Boccaccio called Pavia "the city of a hundred towers." Influential families built more than one hundred so-called noble towers to demonstrate their power and prosperity to everyone else. Only a few of these tall towers are still intact, such as the 197-foot (60 meters) Torre

Belcredi from the thirteenth century, or the Torre del Maino with its 167 feet (51 meters).

The city of towers is located on the banks of the Ticino River and has in essence kept its medieval image. Built in the fourteenth century, the Castello Visconteo, with its imposing towers, is now home to the city museum exhibiting finds from ancient times to the twentieth century. Masterpieces by Giovanni Bellini, Antonio da Correggio, Antonello da Messina, Giovanni Battista Tiepolo, and many other great names in Italian art history are on display in the Pinacoteca Malaspina, a small but fine collection of paintings.

GENUINE CHURCH TREASURES

There are three places of worship travelers must absolutely visit. San Pietro in Ciel d'Oro is one of the most beautiful examples of Romanesque architecture in Northern Italy. Above the altar is the Arca di Sant'Agostino; the skull and bones of St. Augustine are said to have been enshrined here, in Pavia, in the eighth century. Santa Maria del Carmine is considered to be one of the most beautiful examples of Gothic architecture influenced by northern European styles, which have been widely employed in Lombardy. Its construction began in 1375. The interior is a kind of art museum. Especially moving is the painting by baroque painter Sebastiano Ricci from 1694.

San Michele Maggiore, whose foundations were set by the Langobards, is the most impressive of Pavia's churches. It was the site of various emperors' coronations, including that of Holy Roman Emperor Frederick Barbarossa. This church, too, features simple, yet elegant and unadulterated Romanesque traits both on the outside and inside, without the distracting additions of later centuries. The cathedral, on the other hand, is a masterpiece of the

OPPOSITE: PAVIA IS NOT ON THE LIST OF TOP DESTINATIONS FOR THE MASSES SO ITS PRETTY OLD TOWN CAN EASILY BE EXPLORED IN A RELAXED WAY. *BELOW*: MANY OF ITS MASTERPIECES ORIGINATED IN ITS ARTISTIC HEYDAY, FROM THE FOURTEENTH TO THE SIXTEENTH CENTURIES.

Renaissance, built in 1488. The famous architect Donato Bramante is said to have designed the crypt.

The Strada Nuova, the main promenade of this town of 73,000 inhabitants, draws an almost straight line from the Castello Visconteo to the river. To the left and right, the Strada is lined with magnificent buildings such as the Teatro Fraschini from the late eighteenth century, the old university, churches, palaces, and the former hospital, Ospedale San Matteo, founded in 1449. Speaking of strolling along the promenade: Pavia's old town is almost entirely traffic-free, and its numerous inviting cafés, bars, and stores are the perfect places to spend time.

UNCHANGED FOR CENTURIES

In 1376, construction began for the Certosa di Pavia, the Carthusian charter house, the church, and the mausoleum of the Visconti family. The result is an elegant building in the high Gothic style, decorated with early Renaissance design elements. The ornate façade dates back to the fifteenth century. Inside, murals glorify the deeds of the princely family, the Visconti of Milan. The crucifixes and other religious works of art were mostly made by regional master craftspeople of the late fifteenth century. The two cloisters, the smaller Chiostro Piccolo and the larger Chiostro Grande, also date to the same period. The Certosa is a fifteen-minute drive to the north of Pavia.

LEARN MORE
Pavia: www.visitpavia.com
Pinacoteca di Malaspina:
http://malaspina.museicivici.pavia.it/
Certosa di Pavia: www.certosadipavia.it

MANTUA – THE FAVORITE OF THE HOUSE OF GONZAGA

COUNTS, COLLECTIONS, AND COLOSSI

A total of three lakes surround this architectural gem of a city, which is especially enchanting in bad weather, in the fog, and when it drizzles. Strollers will discover the charm of bygone centuries at many of Mantua's corners.

Lago Superiore, Lago Inferiore, and Lago di Mezzo ("Upper," "Lower," and "Middle" Lakes, respectively): three bodies of water surround the small but historically very rich old town of Mantua. People lived here as early as 6,000 years ago—as the discovery of the so-called "Lovers of Valdaro" testifies. This ancient pair of skeletons was unearthed in a Neolithic tomb near the church of San Giorgio in 2007. But it was only with the arrival of the Romans that the town, founded by the Etruscans, developed into a city. By the way, its name derives from the Greek prophetess Manto.

FROM GONZAGA TO HABSBURG

Mantua received its present appearance from the once powerful Gonzaga, a noble family appreciative of art that owed its political rise to the Holy Roman Emperors. These promoted the local counts to influential dukes. After much historical turmoil, Mantua eventually became Austrian—and remained part of the Habsburg Empire until the mid-nineteenth century, with only one short interlude during Napoleon's reign. During this time, Mantua developed into a quiet and rather provincial small town. The picturesque old town surrounded by water is so densely packed with first-class preserved buildings that it has been featured on the UNESCO World Heritage List since 2008. An important note for visitors: this town of 50,000 inhabitants offers enough attractions to fill two whole days of sightseeing.

IN THE BRIDAL CHAMBER

For a long time, Mantua's political center was the mighty Palazzo Ducale. It was the site from which the Gonzaga ruled their microstate. Built in the fourteenth century, and constantly expanded, this palace now features almost 450 rooms! One of

OPPOSITE: **UNCHANGED FOR CENTURIES: THE VIEW OF MANTUA'S OLD TOWN.**
THIS PAGE: **TEATRO SCIENTIFICO TRANSLATES AS "SCIENTIFIC THEATER," AND, INDEED, IT SERVES AS A BAROQUE STAGE AND BALLROOM FOR THE ROYAL VIRGILIAN ACADEMY OF SCIENCE AND ARTS.**

these is adorned with the most famous frescoes in the history of Italian art. Renaissance painter Andrea Mantegna created the Camera degli sposi, the "bridal chamber," in the middle of the fifteenth century. Ornate paintings cover all the wall surfaces. The ceiling fresco depicts the gates of heaven, from which people and cherubs look down at the observer.

Only a few steps away is the Basilica of Sant'Andrea, designed in the late fifteenth century by Renaissance star architect Leon Battista Alberti. However, the large place of worship was not completed until the baroque era. The Turin architect Juvarra created the dome in the eighteenth century. The church has an impressive interior: three large and various minor side chapels branch off the central nave and are adorned with artworks in a triumph of luxuriance! Giulio Romano gave the finishing touches to the medieval cathedral, which was rebuilt in the style of the Roman baroque—that is, in a lavishly decorated way. The court painter, architect, and master builder took inspiration from St. Peter's Basilica for his reconstruction project.

FROM OPERATIONS TO OPERA

One of the most bizarre and unique buildings in all of Italy is the Teatro Scientifico. Its name, "Scientific Theater," recalls the Renaissance period when medical practitioners performed operations in front of a live audience. Various historical universities in Italy still feature these types of "operating theaters." The Mantuan Teatro Scientifico appears to the visitor as a kind of opera house. It was designed by Antonio Galli Bibiena, the most famous stage designer of the Rococo era. The theater was inaugurated in 1769, a gem with four rows of boxes, crystal chandeliers, and golden decorations as well as—in keeping with the dominant Rococo style—plenty of scrolling curves.

A not-quite 14-year-old Mozart performed his compositions here in December 1769. The interior of this theater has remained unchanged to this day—a rarity, even in Italy.

OPPOSITE: IN MANTUA'S OLD TOWN, RESIDENTIAL AND COMMERCIAL BUILDINGS HUG THE BASILICA. LEFT: THE STATE ROOMS OF THE PALAZZO DEL TE ARE LAVISHLY DECORATED WITH FRESCOES.

GORGEOUS PALAZZO DEL TE

In the south of the old town, in easy walking distance along the almost dead-straight Via Roma, which merges into the Via Principe Amedeo, is this masterpiece of Renaissance architecture. Giulio Romano, a pupil of Raphael's, designed this summer residence. Because of its location on the island Isola del Teieto, it is simply known as Palazzo del Te or Palazzo Te. It is one of the most beautiful examples of sixteenth-century Italian architecture.

Late Renaissance painters, including Rinaldo Mantovano, embellished the square house—with its cloistered courtyard and various gardens—with striking frescoes. The depictions show banquets with Greek gods and goddesses as well as simply incredible life-size horses and larger-than-life giants. These paintings rendered speechless contemporary visitors, such as Emperor Charles V, when he was hosted by Federico II Gonzaga in 1530. Nowadays, the Palazzo del Te is almost empty: Mantua was looted in 1630. The only things left were the frescoes. When walking through the vast painted halls, many visitors feel as if they are strolling through a huge comic strip. A few of the rooms are reserved for the municipal museum. Connoisseurs of old coins will find the numismatic collection interesting; it comprises 400 historical pieces of money from the early fourteenth to the eighteenth century. A very evocative part of the Palazzo Te complex is the Casino della Grotta. You have the opportunity to wander through a suite of rooms, arranged around a loggia and a grotto.

Strolling through Mantua, you will necessarily come across the Museo Diocesano Francesco Gonzaga. Instead of world-famous masterpieces, a collection of gold work and paintings from the late Middle Ages to the baroque awaits the visitor favorably disposed towards religious art.

AROUND MANTUA ON WATERWAYS

The "barcaroli," Mantua's boatmen and women, offer delightful excursions not only on the lakes but also on the Mincio River, which flows to the west of the city. The view of historical Mantua seen from the water is particularly beautiful. Not a single modern building disrupts the skyline, which instead resembles an ancient painting. The Mincio boatmen also offer tours, for example from Mantua to Rivalta, one of the most famous nature reserves in Northern Italy. Another appealing trip is a visit to the pilgrimage church Santuario della Beata Vergine delle Grazie near Curtatone, an old fishing village, where director Bernardo Bertolucci shot his drama film *1900* in the middle of a bucolic, swampy landscape teaming with herons and many species of waterfowl.

LEARN MORE
Mantua: www.mantova.com
Palazzo Te: www.palazzote.it
Barcaroli Tours: www.fiumemincio.it

THE PALAZZO DEL TE IS ONE OF THE MOST IMPRESSIVE RENAISSANCE BUILDINGS IN NORTHERN ITALY.

MONTAGNANA – THE WALLED-IN WONDER
PERFECT PROTECTION

Montagnana is little known, even among Italians. That's a real shame, because this small town has something very special to offer: there are very few places in Europe that have been protected by such an impressive fortified wall for centuries.

The dimensions alone are awe-inspiring: the walls are 21 to 26 feet (6.5 to 8 meters) tall and 37 to 39 inches (96 to 100 centimeters) thick. A total of twenty-four perimeter towers are dotted around the wall, at approximately 200-foot intervals (60 meters). Each of the fortified towers measures between 55 and 62 feet (17 to 19 meters) in height. A passage inside the city walls allows visitors to walk around the entire old town. The intramural town center is enclosed in a quadrilateral of about 1,970 by 985 feet (600 by 300 meters). This truly epochal city wall protects Montagnana in the province of Padua, and it is one of the best preserved of its kind worldwide—and one of the best illustrations of medieval military architecture. It was the Carraresi family who had the first fortifications built in the mid-thirteenth century. At that time, the town was located on the border between Padua, governed by the Carraresis, and their enemies, the Scaligeri family, who ruled neighboring Verona.

FORGOTTEN BY HISTORY

These days, Montagnana appears as an odd, quiet, and romantic place, a bit cut off from the world. Fewer than 9,000 people live here. Founded by the Romans, the settlement was part of the Republic of Venice between 1405 and 1707.

Yet there is a lot to discover on a tour of Montagnana. The fact that the town has been a provincial backwater for centuries means that many of the historical structures have remained intact. In

OPPOSITE: **TO THIS DAY, MONTAGNANA IS COMPLETELY SURROUNDED BY A MEDIEVAL CITY WALL.** *LEFT*: **THE OLD TOWN IS LIT UP LIKE A STAGE SET AFTER DARK.**

addition to the medieval city walls, these sites include the network of old streets that weave through the city center, as well as the historical buildings, all of which date from the period between the Renaissance and the nineteenth century.

The cathedral from the late fifteenth century bears the trademark of the late Gothic style and hides a precious painting: a transfiguration by the Venetian star painter Paolo Veronese. Another painting depicts the Battle of Lepanto, in which a Christian army defeated Muslim attackers in 1571. The interior church walls are adorned with frescoes, including one that was only recently attributed to one of the greatest artists of the Italian Renaissance: Giorgione.

A WALK THROUGH THE OLD TOWN

The square in front of the cathedral is lined with multiple palaces. The town hall in the nearby Via Carrarese is the work of Renaissance architect Michele Sanmicheli, dating from 1538. The Ospedale di Santa Maria, an early hospital located in the Via dei Montagnana, is said to have been founded by the Templars. Just outside the old town is one of the masterpieces of Renaissance all-round talent Andrea Palladio, whose style influenced the architecture of country mansions for several centuries. Villa Pisani from the 1550s is an extremely elegant rectangular building with little decoration. Master Palladio's aim was to establish a direct link with his architectural role models of ancient Rome.

Unsurprisingly, Montagnana has two fortified castles. Rocca degli Alberi from the fourteenth century solely served to defend the city. Castello di San Zeno, on the other hand, was inhabited by the dukes of Este, among others. Both complexes are well preserved and provide a nice impression of grand medieval architecture.

A CELEBRATION OF FREEDOM

Since 1977, on every first Sunday in September—when good weather is more or less guaranteed—locals celebrate the so-called Palio dei 10 Comuni del Montagnanese. Residents of the old town, but also those living in the neighborhoods outside the city walls, attend the fair. Parades and competitions in historical garb commemorate the end of the tyranny of Ezzelino III, the Terrible. On this day of celebration, almost the entire old town is decked out as if it were a set for a medieval movie—complete with the enticing scents of local delicacies wafting through the streets. In the evening, fireworks light up the Rocca degli Alberi.

LEARN MORE
Montagnana: www.visitmontagnana.it
Palio dei 10 Comuni: www.palio10comuni.it

THIS PAGE: PARMA IS HOME TO ONE OF THE MOST BEAUTIFUL HISTORICAL OPERA HOUSES IN ITALY.
OPPOSITE: THE CENTRAL SQUARE, THE CHURCH, AND ITS BAPTISTERY ARE ALL LAID OUT IN THE ELEGANT ROMANESQUE STYLE OF NORTHERN ITALY.

PARMA – SOMETHING FOR THE EYES, THE EARS, AND THE PALATE
CITY OF SENSUAL DELIGHTS

Ham, cheese, and pasta; the well-kept and restored old town; a great music scene including a famous theater; and a lot of art—the city on the ancient Via Aemilia is a place of many delights. Gourmets and cultural aficionados will get their money's worth in Parma.

The city's secret center is not a cathedral, a basilica, or an impressive palace. The town's focal point—already unique in Catholic Italy—is a place of music and delights, with the Teatro Regio as its temple. Music fans travel from all over Italy and farther afield to attend the operas and concerts performed here. Duchess Maria Luisa decided in the early nineteenth century that the theater built in 1689 was simply too old. She wanted something modern in its place, so she had a monastery demolished and a new, larger theater built with a 1,800-seat auditorium. On May 16, 1829, it was officially opened with the opera *Zaire* by the Sicilian Vincenzo Bellini—a piece especially commissioned by the music lovers of Parma.

THE MUSICAL CENTER

The Teatro Regio was later renovated and now appears as a masterpiece of neoclassical architecture, housing one of the most beautiful historical auditoriums in Europe. The ceiling bears the weight of a huge chandelier, which has been in operation since 1853. The Regio, as it is called in Parma, has always provided the stage for noteworthy performances. It is here where the greatest of composers present their works and the most important soloists show off their abilities. Maria Callas and Mirella Freni, Renata Scotto and Luciano Pavarotti have graced the stage of the Regio. A tour of the stage or, better still, an evening at a concert or the opera is a key part of any visit to Parma—just as several restaurant outings are a must.

The "cucina parmigiana" is one of a kind. The city's ancient and famous cuisine has found radical followers who are convinced that any trip to Parma is worth it for the food alone. There is enough to taste for at least a whole week's stay. More than ten local starters are considered to be culinary classics. They each almost exclusively focus on one particular pasta shape. There are anolini and tortelli (those stuffed with pumpkin cream are particularly delightful). Then there are gnocchi and tagliolini with seductive Culatello ham. La Rosa di Parma is a main dish consisting of veal with Parma ham and grated Parma cheese. Delicious! Truly vast is the selection of local sausages and sliced cold meats and cheeses. Parma ham is known all over the world—but it is tastiest when it has been freshly sliced. Alongside all of these culinary delights, opt for a glass of the local tipple, the lively red Lambrusco.

You can find a variety of traditional restaurants with guaranteed local food all over the city. So there is plenty of choice for the almost 200,000 inhabitants and their guests!

THE RELIGIOUS PARMA

Not far from the musical center of the city is its religious hub. The cathedral is one of the main buildings of Romanesque architecture in Northern Italy. Neither baroque nor other additions disturb the façade's plain but elegant architecture or the Gothic bell tower. The interior houses significant pieces of sacred art. In the 1520s, the painter Antonio da Correggio created the *Assumption of the*

LEFT: PARMA IS HOME TO THE GALLERIA NAZIONALE, ONE OF THE RICHEST ART COLLECTIONS IN NORTHERN ITALY. *ABOVE*: EVERYONE KNOWS PARMA HAM, BUT IT TASTES EVEN BETTER WHEN SAMPLED IN SITU.

Virgin, an especially vivid fresco. The Romanesque artist Benedetto Antelami, one of the greatest sculptors of his time, created a bas-relief in 1178 depicting the Deposition of Christ. Next to the cathedral—and spatially separated from it in the classic fashion of Romanesque-Gothic Northern Italy—is the Battistero, the large baptistery. Built between 1196 and 1270, the octagonal building features five stories decorated with columns. Inside, medieval sculptures symbolize the months and seasons as well as the zodiac signs.

Right behind the cathedral's apse is the great Renaissance church of San Giovanni Evangelista. It is famous for its Correggio fresco cycle. It depicts the life of John the Evangelist in a simultaneously haunting and pretty colorful way. Between these two places of worship is the Storica Spezieria di San Giovanni Evangelista. The historical pharmacy, founded in 1201 and in operation until 1766, has been restored in recent years and can be visited.

ONE PALACE, TWO MUSEUMS

Just a stone's throw away from the cathedral and the Teatro Regio is the impressive Palazzo della Pilotta, which used to be the political center of the city for several centuries. It was the seat of the Farnese family, who ruled over Parma. The palace was built between 1583 and 1622 in an elegant transition style between the late Renaissance and the early baroque periods. Two museums are housed in the large palazzo.

The National Archaeological Museum, founded by Filippo I di Borbone in 1760, exhibits excavation finds discovered around Parma in the eighteenth century and later. The so-called "Tabula Alimentaria" is particularly noteworthy; the largest remaining bronze plaque from Roman antiquity measures 4.5 by 9.4 feet (1.38 by 2.86 meters) and dates from the time of Emperor Nerva—that is, from the first century CE.

The Galleria Nazionale is the most important museum in Parma; it's a treasure trove of paintings. Major works from the thirteenth to the eighteenth centuries are exhibited here, including works by Canaletto, Correggio, Parmigianino, Murillo, Van Dyck, Tiepolo, and many others. A visit is a must for art lovers! The museum also includes the bizarre Teatro Farnese from 1617. It is one of the most peculiar and surprising theaters in the world: a huge wooden amphitheater with a roof.

Parma's historical center is pretty small. In addition to a couple of squares, romantic alleyways with chic stores (especially with delicatessen in abundance) attract visitors—not to mention all those restaurants that make a day in Parma just perfect. Or, indeed, a second and a third day . . .

VISITING THE MASTER

About a thirty-minute drive northwest of Parma is the town of Roncole Verdi, where Giuseppe Verdi, Italy's most famous composer, lived. You can visit his birthplace here, a sacred pilgrimage site for opera lovers. It also used to be the location of his summer residence, Villa Verdi (also open to visitors), with the maestro's private chambers and full of venerable relics. The inventory also includes furnishings from the Milanese hotel in which Verdi died. A further nine-minute drive away is Busseto. At the master's place of study is the Teatro Giuseppe Verdi, which hosts a Verdi season every year. Very charming is the Villa Pallavicino, a large baroque complex with magnificent interiors, some halls of which are dedicated to the composer—a note for Verdi fans.

LEARN MORE
Parma: www.parmawelcome.it
Galleria Nazionale: www.complessopilotta.it
Teatro Regio: www.teatroregioparma.it

THIS PAGE: CONTEMPORARY ART IN THE HISTORICAL STREETS OF FERRARA.
OPPOSITE: PERHAPS THE MOST BEAUTIFUL SETTING: A VIEW OF THE LOCAL CASTLE AT NIGHT, SURROUNDED BY MOATS.

FERRARA – EMILIA-ROMAGNA FOR ROMANTICS
A RENAISSANCE DREAM

Ferrara is undoubtedly one of the artistic strongholds of Italy. It was the professional home of painters such as Piero della Francesca, writers such as Ariosto, and musicians such as Girolamo Frescobaldi. The German historian Jacob Burckhardt called Ferrara "Europe's first modern city."

Many film and literature lovers know Ferrara; anyone who has read Giorgio Bassani's 1962 novel *The Gardens of the Finzi-Continis* or watched the 1970 movie of the same name starring Helmut Berger and Fabio Testi as protagonists knows that Ferrara is a sleepy city full of art. The story tells of a rich Jewish family that was excluded from society after the introduction of the racial laws in Italy in 1938, and later deported by the Germans. The film made Ferrara world famous among cinema enthusiasts.

The mood that marks the novel and the movie—that of a small town in the region of Emilia-Romagna that marches to a different beat—still prevails today. Ferrara's atmosphere is one of its most attractive features, so you should stay over here for at least one night. There is plenty to visit.

CURIOUS CATHEDRAL
The cathedral at the central Piazza Cattedrale is undoubtedly one of the most extraordinary churches in all of Italy. It features unadulterated

Romanesque architecture, combined with elements from the early Renaissance. The marble steeple was built in the sixteenth century. Inside and in the Museo del Duomo, visitors will get to see much sacred art: paintings, sculptures, and tapestries by important artists, such as Guercino and the sculptor Jacopo della Quercia. A loggia adorns one side of the cathedral. For centuries, goods were sold here. And, to this day, a market takes place on this side of the main church.

A few perfectly straight streets run through Ferrara that are lined with magnificent buildings. Walking along these, you will notice archways and covered alleys; in medieval times, in order to save space, houses were built across streets as well.

The Palazzo Schifanoia is considered one of the most beautiful buildings in the city. The building from the fifteenth century houses the Museo Civico. It is a rich museum, since the d'Este, who had long ruled Ferrara, were one of the families most appreciative of art during the Italian Renaissance. Acting as patrons, they attracted many artists. The museum exhibits one of the most important fresco cycles in Northern Italy. The Hall of the Months shows large-scale allegorical depictions of the calendar months. They were created by various Ferrara artists during the second half of the fifteenth century.

The archaeological museum, another art history delight, is located not far away in the Palazzo di Ludovico il Moro. The palace was built in 1495 according to plans by the Renaissance architect Biagio Rossetti. It exhibits sarcophagi and works of art by the Etruscans and the Romans.

The palaces of Ferrara belonged not only to members of the nobility but also to wealthy

LEFT: **A FAÇADE LIKE A CUT DIAMOND: THE PALAZZO DEI DIAMANTI.** *ABOVE*: **A MEDIEVAL MADONNA ABOVE THE NORTHERN PORTAL OF THE CATHEDRAL.**

merchants. Several of these line the lively Corso della Giovecca. Open to visitors is the Palazzina di Marfisa from 1559, the former residence of a noblewoman, which includes antique furniture and musical instruments.

RELIGIOUS CONFLICTS IN THE FAMILY

The secular center of Ferrara is concentrated around the Castello Estense, a moated castle in the middle of the city with fortifications from the fourteenth century and painted halls. The view of the city from the Loggia degli Aranci is simply stunning. A curious sight to behold is the so-called Cappella calvinista. This richly decorated chapel without any kind of pictorial representations used to belong to Renata of France, the second daughter of King Louis XII. Although her husband, Ercole II d'Este, was a staunch Catholic, she remained a committed Protestant and supporter of the reformer Calvin.

A DIAMOND OF A PALACE

Just north of the Castello and within easy walking distance—like all sites in Ferrara—lies an architectural gem: the Palazzo dei Diamanti, which is certainly one of the most elegant buildings from the time of the d'Este family and a major work of the Italian Renaissance. Designed by Biagio Rossetti in the late fifteenth century, the palace was completed in the sixteenth century. The Pinacoteca Nazionale is located here. Masterpieces by Cosmè Tura, Dosso Dossi, Vittore Carpaccio, Gentile da Fabriano, and Andrea Mantegna are displayed here in one of the most important collections of paintings in Northern Italy. There are also Byzantine murals from various churches in Ferrara. The building owes its name to the peculiar design of its façade, which—according to the architect's wishes—was composed of 12,600 individual marble blocks. Their fronts were not placed to display their flat side as usual, but rather to form a pyramid shape, thus recalling cut diamonds. The diamond was the trademark of Duke Ercole I. d'Este. Today, the Palazzo hosts interesting art exhibitions.

A JEWISH CITY

For centuries, many Jewish citizens called Ferrara their home. While the Este and other ruling families were not staunch defenders of the Jews, they let them be, knowing full well that this segment of the population contributed a great deal to the city's prosperity. The members of Ferrara's Jewish community were granted a number of freedoms.

The National Museum of Italian Judaism and the Shoah, called MEIS, has only been in existence for a handful of years but is well worth a visit. The economic and cultural contributions the Jewish population made to Ferrara are the focus of this museum. The end of the peaceful coexistence between Christians and Jews in Ferrara also features here: the ending was as abrupt as the writer Giorgio Bassani described in his novel.

THE STREET OF ARCHES

The Via delle Volte, the street of arches, is about 1.2 miles (2 kilometers) long and is a curious stretch, even by Ferrara's standards. Visitors will stroll past gloomy old buildings under arches that bear the weight of several-story-high buildings. People used to build in this way to make ultimate use of space. The result is a tunnel effect that is extremely alluring on dark days when rain or fog have set in—which is not a rarity in Ferrara. At night, when the streets are illuminated in a golden yellow glow, the Via delle Volte seems mysterious. Some of the arches were built to allow merchants to access their warehouses and stores straight from their homes, without having to walk along the dirty streets of their time.

LEARN MORE

Ferrara: www.ferrarainfo.com
MEIS: www.meisweb.it
Palazzo dei Diamanti: www.palazzodiamanti.it

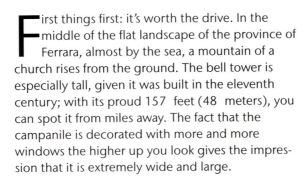

POMPOSA – THE HIDDEN ABBEY
A CHURCH IN THE MIDDLE OF NOWHERE

These days, there are only few places left in densely populated Italy where great cultural masterpieces can be found in deserted settings. The Abbazia di Pomposa is one of them. Ferrara and Ravenna are each around an hour's drive away.

First things first: it's worth the drive. In the middle of the flat landscape of the province of Ferrara, almost by the sea, a mountain of a church rises from the ground. The bell tower is especially tall, given it was built in the eleventh century; with its proud 157 feet (48 meters), you can spot it from miles away. The fact that the campanile is decorated with more and more windows the higher up you look gives the impression that it is extremely wide and large.

EARLY CHRISTIAN GEM
The Abbazia di Pomposa is a Benedictine abbey in the province of Ferrara. The religious complex was first mentioned in records in the ninth century. It was erected on the remains of an early Christian chapel dating to the sixth century. The monastery complex at the mouth of the Po River was so large and impressive because in the Middle Ages the monks here were wealthy and powerful and owned land throughout Italy, which afforded them plenty of profits.

The monastery benefited from its location on an extremely fertile island, surrounded by two arms of the Po, and its proximity to the Roman trade route Strada romea, which connected Venice with Ravenna and Rome. Following their motto "ora et labora" ("pray and work"), the monks literally laid the groundwork, both in agricultural and cultural terms. One of the most important personalities

among the brothers was a monk named Guido, also known as Guido of Arezzo. He is considered the inventor of modern musical notation.

Over the centuries, the Po River changed its course, malaria spread, and the smaller waterways around the abbey silted up. The monastery lost its importance—so much so that the complex was closed in 1653. Nowadays, it belongs to the Italian state—which, by the way, as only very few Italians know, has taken on ownership of around 20 percent of all places of worship in Italy since the country's unification in the mid-nineteenth century. The monastery's church is dedicated to St. Mary. It is a basilica whose architectural style recalls that of nearby Ravenna. It dates from the eighth and ninth centuries and was considerably expanded later on.

FRESCOES AND SACRED ART

The interior, with its plain, medieval look and only few decorations, exudes great charisma. Its only notable features are the well-preserved fourteenth-century murals by Vitale da Bologna and his workshop.

The best-kept building of the former monastery complex from the eleventh century is the chapter hall, embellished with frescoes dating from the fourteenth century with motifs in the style of a successor of Giotto's. You can also visit the refectory, which houses the most important murals of the entire monastery complex. Since the monks were not allowed to chat during meal times, the idea was probably that they should at least have something to look at while eating.

The upper floor of the monastery is home to the Pomposa Museum. Worth seeing are the beautiful

OPPOSITE: **A CHURCH, A BELL TOWER, AND A FEW BUILDINGS ENGULFED BY NATURE: THE ABBAZIA DI POMPOSA.** BELOW: **THE INTERIOR OF THE ABBEY CHURCH IS PAINTED ALL OVER WITH MURALS.**

precious sacred works from the Byzantine period—that is, from the seventh and eighth centuries.

The monks' tasks were to manage their wealth and dispense justice. They did this from their hub at the Palazzo della Ragione. This administrative building, which dates back to the twelfth century and was renovated in the fourteenth, towers over the Basilica of Santa Maria; it served to demonstrate the abbey's feudal powers.

FOREST ANIMALS

The 2,066-acre (836 hectares) nature reserve Riserva Naturale Bosco della Mesola is located on an estuary between the mainland and the sea, with forests and marshes that are no more than 10 feet (3 meters) above sea level. Over the centuries, nature has reclaimed the former agricultural land belonging to the monks. Around three hundred different species of mammals live in this paradise today, including the now rare Mesola deer. From March to October, an electric bus takes visitors through the park, including to places frequented by the deer. There is also a huge variety of bird species, as well as an impressive range of snakes and reptiles. Hikers are therefore advised to wear sturdy footwear or boots.

LEARN MORE
Pomposa: www.ferraraterraeacqua.it
Riserva Naturale Bosco della Mesola:
www.ferraraterraeacqua.it

GENOA – THE BYPASSED METROPOLIS
UNDERRATED BEAUTY

It is one of the most important port cities in Europe featuring one of the largest and most beautiful old towns in Italy—and that is saying something! And yet, many travelers only come to Genoa to take the ferry to Corsica or Sardinia.

The medieval prince of poetry, Petrarca, called Genoa "la superba": the proud one. This is unsurprising, since the history of this port city, which was once one of the most important maritime powers of the Middle Ages, is something to be proud of. It is an adventurous story in which rich and powerful noble families played a decisive role, governed by an elected doge—just like Venice, Genoa's great rival in the Mediterranean.

Located directly on the Ligurian Sea, Genoa was built on the steep slopes of the Apennine Mountains. Ergo, you have to be a good walker to explore the old town. The historical center is crisscrossed with splendid baroque streets, the so-called "Strade Nuove," which are lined with Renaissance and baroque palaces. Genoa's old town is so precious that UNESCO granted it World Heritage Site designation in 2006.

GREEK BEGINNINGS
It was probably the Greeks who first settled here—a Greek cemetery from the fourth century BCE testifies to that. The Hellenes were followed by the conquering and entrepreneurial Carthaginians and finally the Romans. In the Middle Ages, the port city prospered in an unprecedented way. It was ruled by patricians, canny merchants, and warriors who were skilled in driving out the Saracens that kept threatening the city from the sea.

OPPOSITE: **ITALY'S LARGEST OLD TOWN IS LOCATED IN THE PORT CITY OF GENOA.** *THIS PAGE:* **ITS GORGEOUS BAROQUE PALACES, SUCH AS THE PALAZZO DORIA-SPINOLA, ARE ON A PAR WITH THOSE IN VENICE AND ROME.**

Money, power, and pride led to the emergence of a "crowned republic," as in the Venetian Lagoon. The patricians—the representatives of the most renowned families—elected a doge to rule alongside a council. Under this government, Genoa rose to become an international trading power with hubs in Casablanca, Portugal, and the Canary Islands. It was regularly at war with other Italian naval powers, with Venice, Pisa, and Amalfi.

MONEY GOVERNED GENOA

As in almost all the Italian city-states of the Middle Ages and the Renaissance, well-functioning finances formed Genoa's economic backbone. Banks such as the Banco di San Giorgio gained a lot of influence. Money was abundant, and—especially in the seventeenth century—the patricians and noble families showed off their interest in art. Very much following the trend of their time, they wanted to demonstrate their wealth. And so the Genoese stopped scrimping and started spending.

Beginning in the sixteenth century, new roads were built within the still-existent defensive fortifications, which had been erected on the mountain ridges around Genoa. These "new roads," the Strade Nuove, were designed to be representative thoroughfares. Because of this, visitors can still marvel at a whole battery of baroque palaces in the Via Garibaldi and the Via Balbi, with magnificent façades that hide quiet courtyards and richly appointed state rooms.

LEFT: ENTIRE STREETS ARE LINED WITH PALACES, ONE AFTER ANOTHER—SUCH AS IN THE VIA BALBI. *ABOVE*: THE HISTORICAL LIGHTHOUSE IS THE HIGHEST IN ALL OF ITALY. *OPPOSITE*: THE ELEGANT FAÇADES OF NOBLE PALACES, SUCH AS THE PALAZZO REALE, CONCEAL ABUNDANT ART COLLECTIONS.

WONDERFUL COLLECTIONS OF PAINTINGS

One of the most important palaces in this city of 575,000 inhabitants is the Palazzo Ducale. It dates back to the thirteenth century, though a devastating fire meant the building had to be entirely rebuilt in the late eighteenth century. After a period of incomprehensible neglect of important historical monuments in the old town, the most significant historical buildings began to be restored from the ground up in the 1990s. Since then, the most beautiful palaces have been restored to their former glory, including the Palazzo Spinola. It once belonged to one of the most powerful doge families of Genoa: the Spinola. Its façade is richly decorated with stucco and bears testament to this being a typical Genoese baroque palace. The palace is home to the National Gallery of Art, featuring major works by painters such as Antonello da Messina, Guido Reni, Anthonis van Dyck, and many others. Van Dyck was a popular portrait painter in baroque Genoa. Every single noble family made sure to find the money to pose for this star portraitist.

WHITE AND RED PALACES

The Palazzo Bianco in the Via Garibaldi houses the treasures of the Galleria di Palazzo Bianco, a collection of extremely valuable paintings by Magnasco, Veronese, Rubens, and, of course, Van Dyck. The Palazzo Rosso, in its immediate vicinity, was built in the seventeenth century and exhibits the results of the inhabitants' passion for collecting in the Galleria di Palazzo Rosso. Here, too, masterpieces are on display, with works by Titian, Tintoretto, Caravaggio, and Dürer. The list of beautiful noble residences also includes the Palazzo Tursi from the sixteenth century, the Palazzo Reale dating from the seventeenth century with a remarkable gallery, and, of course, the Palazzo Doria Pamphilj. This city palace is certainly one of the most magnificent aristocratic residences in Genoa. The famous admiral, politician, and aristocrat Andrea Doria, one of the heroes of Genoese history, expanded this palace in the first half of the sixteenth century. He added loggias that afforded a view of the sea and had Perino del Vaga paint the interiors with magnificent murals.

Genoa's old town offers churches worth visiting. These include the Romanesque church of San Matteo from the twelfth to the thirteenth centuries and the grandiose St. Lawrence Cathedral, consecrated by Pope Gelasius II in 1118. The building was not completed until 1522. It displays the characteristic marker of Ligurian medieval architecture: namely, a façade consisting of alternating layers of black and white stone.

THE GENUINE HOLY GRAIL

The severe medieval interior conceals two treasures. A chapel from the fifteenth century devoted to John the Baptist displays a fascinating Madonna by Andrea Sansovino. The second treasure, the Museum of the Treasury of Saint Lawrence, displays a real rarity that you won't see anywhere else: Genoese tradition has it that the Sacro Catino, a green glass dish, was the true Holy Grail—the vessel from which Jesus Christ was said to have drunk during the Last Supper.

In the church of San Donato hangs a magnificent triptych, a three-part altarpiece by Joos van Cleve from the early sixteenth century. The church of Santa Maria di Castello, dating from the early Renaissance period, boasts several interesting courtyards and beautiful murals dating back to the fifteenth century in the adjacent Dominican convent. After so much art, it is fun to just drift through the alleyways and boulevards of Genoa. One of these is the Via Balbi, with its beautiful city palaces.

A MEGA LIGHTHOUSE

Perhaps the most beautiful viewpoint of Genoa is the so-called Righi. The most convenient way to reach the suburb on the hill, at 984 feet (300 meters), is by taking the funicular, or "funicolare." The Righi opens up a breathtaking panorama over the entire old town and to the sea.

In plain sight is also La Lanterna. This is one of the oldest and tallest lighthouses in the world. From its base, it measures 384 feet (117 meters), while the actual tower is 253 feet (77 meters) tall. Its predecessor was erected in the twelfth century; La Lanterna, as it presents itself today, dates back to the first half of the sixteenth century.

Below, right by the sea, is the famous Aquarium of Genoa, which shows the largest number of marine life-forms in all of Europe. Its 290,626 square feet (27,000 square meters) let you explore more than seventy marine seascapes

OPPOSITE: **THE PICTURESQUE FISHING VILLAGE OF BOCCADASSE IS LOCATED IN THE IMMEDIATE VICINITY OF THE METROPOLIS.** *LEFT:* **GENOA'S AQUARIUM IS ITALY'S LARGEST.**

with more than six hundred species from all the world's oceans, featuring more than 15,000 creatures. Most visitors marvel at the panes of these tanks teeming with jellyfish and tropical sea creatures. In a cylindrical, almost 20-foot-high (6 meters) pool designed to imitate a seashell and called the "grotto of moray eels," visitors can watch these animals at close proximity. A remarkable experience!

Another curious—and also rather bizarre—place in Italy's sixth largest city is the famous Cimitero monumentale. A huge cemetery was created in the Staglieno neighborhood in 1835, where the city's leading families had mausoleums built for their family members, lavishly decorated, and embellished.

A STROLL TO BOCCADASSE

An essential part of visiting Genoa is seeing Boccadasse, a picturesque fishing village right by the sea. In 1874, a total of six surrounding villages were incorporated into the city area, including pretty Boccadasse. It can be reached by car in about fifteen minutes from the aquarium. Or you can walk there, along the beautiful Passeggiata a Mare. This path leads along the sea, often very close to the cliffs. The views of the ocean and the coast are just stunning.

On the way to Boccadasse, you will pass San Giuliano d'Albaro, a Gothic church in an idyllic setting on a rocky outcrop towering over cypress trees. Built in 1240, it is worth looking at the murals inside. The Lido d'Albaro, located right by the church, is one of the most charming beaches in Genoa, complete with cafés, restaurants, and viewpoints. This walk is a fine and romantic way to end a day of sightseeing in Genoa.

CINQUE TERRE – ONE PRETTY VILLAGE AFTER ANOTHER

The five neighboring communities, commonly called Cinque Terre, have been a UNESCO World Heritage Site since 1997. This comes as no surprise, since the ancient villages and their terraced vineyards cultivated on the steep slopes along the coast are one of a kind. Even though fishing boats are still rolling gently in the small ports, people here make their living almost exclusively from tourism. The Azzurro hiking trail is very picturesque; it connects the villages with each other and offers panoramic views of the coast and the sea at regular intervals.

LEARN MORE
Genoa: www.visitgenoa.it
Aquarium of Genoa: www.acquariodigenova.it
Genoa's Museums: www.museidigenova.it
Cinque Terre: www.cinqueterre.eu.com

THE OLD TOWN INVITES YOU TO STROLL AND SHOP (*THIS PAGE*)—AND BE SEDUCED BY THE WARES ON OFFER IN THE DELICATESSENS (*OPPOSITE*).

BOLOGNA – THE GREAT UNKNOWN
MADE FOR GOURMETS

The capital of the Emilia-Romagna region is not a major tourist destination. However, Bologna has a lot of visual and culinary delights to offer; it is considered one of the culinary metropolises of Italy.

Italians also call Bologna "la grassa": the fatty one. This moniker does not just refer to the sheer amount of calories or dishes that are hard to digest. The name refers to a type of cuisine that is characterized by gastronomic traditions and customs, as well as recipes that have been handed down over centuries.

Countless dishes are called "alla bolognese"—many more than the widely popular spaghetti. For example, "ragù alla bolognese," tagliatelle pasta, tortellini and lasagna, "spuma di mortadella" (a type of mortadella cream), "cotoletta alla bolognese," and the dessert "crescente bolognese"—which makes you lick every last bit from your fingers—are just a small selection of the local cuisine that alone makes it well worth a visit to this city of 390,000 inhabitants, which also boasts a magnificent historical center.

CULINARY SCIENCES

Historians say Bologna's culinary tradition is closely linked to the university. It is considered one of the oldest in the world, founded in 1088 by a scholar of law called Irnerius, also known as Wernerius. Other researchers date its foundation to 1125. In any case, almost all of the buildings left to be visited today date to the eighteenth century. With more than 730,000 books and manuscripts, the library is one of the most prized in the world.

Culinary scientists maintain that students and professors coming from all over Italy and abroad to Bologna since the Middle Ages has greatly enriched local kitchens. The result is a cuisine that is not only filling but also offers a menu of hearty dishes so delicious that they have written Italian gourmet history. Certainly, Bologna's geographical position will have ensured that many of those who passed through from the north or south have left their gastronomic mark.

MEDIEVAL DOMINANCE

Bononia was founded in the second century BCE, on the Roman Via Aemilia, one of the most important roads of antiquity, which connected the East and the West. Bologna's historic center is a charming mix of the Middle Ages and the baroque period. Any tour should start at the main square, the Piazza Maggiore. Besides a collection of historical palaces that line this square, San Petronio Basilica is worth the trek.

Construction of Bologna's principal church began in the fourteenth century. By 1659, work on one of the most impressive Gothic churches in Italy was complete. The three entrance portals alone are simply breathtaking! The sculptural decorations by Jacopo della Quercia are considered to be one of the main works of the early fifteenth century. The huge interior looks like a museum of sacred art. Almost every one of the chapels features important paintings by the Bologna School, almost all of them dating to the fifteenth and sixteenth centuries.

Also towering over the square is the impressive Palazzo Comunale, Bologna's city hall since the Middle Ages. It received its current appearance in the fifteenth century. The Palazzo houses various art

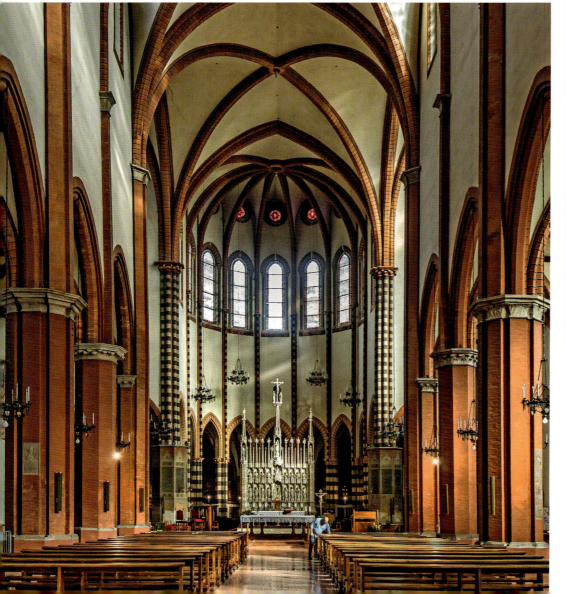

LEFT: **THE BASILICA OF SAN FRANCESCO IS A MASTERPIECE OF GOTHIC AND EARLY RENAISSANCE ARCHITECTURE.** *ABOVE*: **A MARBLE CANDLESTICK. MANY PLACES OF WORSHIP ARE GENUINE ART MUSEUMS.** *OPPOSITE*: **BOLOGNA FROM ABOVE: CHURCHES, PALACES, HISTORICAL RESIDENCES, AND DOMES, SURROUNDED BY ROLLING HILLS.**

collections, such as the Collezioni comunali d'Arte, featuring paintings from the thirteenth to the eighteenth centuries. The center of Piazza Maggiore is marked by the Fontana del Nettuno. The huge Neptune Fountain with bronze sculptures by Renaissance artist Giambologna is considered one of the most important artistic fountains of sixteenth-century Italy.

ANCIENT SKYSCRAPERS

Not far from the main square, two medieval leaning towers rise above the town center. One of them is the almost 322-foot-tall (98 meters) Torre degli Asinelli from the twelfth century. You can reach its top by climbing its 498 steps. The view from the terrace atop is breathtaking. This lopsided tower tilts at an angle of 7.3 feet (2.23 meters). Its neighbor, the 157-foot-tall (48 meters) Torre Garisenda, has an even greater overhang of 10.6 feet (3.22 meters). These are the only two remaining noble towers in Bologna. In the Middle Ages, these were not only found in the "Manhattan of Tuscany," the well-known town of San Gimignano, but across Central and Northern Italy. Unlike in San Gimignano, most of the other towers in Bologna were either demolished or collapsed. In Bologna, these two very impressive examples are the only ones remaining.

The Basilica of San Giacomo Maggiore also dates back to the Middle Ages. Inside, it contains two art history treasures. The Poggi Chapel is a Mannerist masterpiece from the period between the Renaissance and the baroque. It was built by Pellegrino Tibaldi. The square Bentivoglio Chapel has a dome of its own. It was consecrated in 1486 and features murals by Lorenzo Costa.

Near the university, the Pinacoteca Nazionale invites visitors to look at the most important collection of paintings in Bologna—a city not exactly known for its dearth of artworks. It displays paintings from the thirteenth to the eighteenth centuries, including works by important painters such as Giotto, Lorenzo Costa, Annibale Carracci, and Guercino.

CITY OF CHURCHES

It's fun to drift through the historical center—preferably always with a city map in hand, so as to avoid missing out on important ancient monuments along the way. These include the Church of Santa Maria dei Servi. Among much religious art from different centuries, it guards a Maestà (a Holy Virgin, enthroned) by Cimabue. Santo Stefano, on the other hand, is a complex of several medieval buildings, including three churches. It features the Chiostro dei Benedettini, a beautiful courtyard dating to the eleventh century.

The district around the church of San Domenico unites numerous historical buildings from the Renaissance and baroque periods in one place. The Dominican church from the thirteenth century was renovated in the early eighteenth century in the "elegant" style popular back then. Baroque painter Guido Reni left a fresco in the

LEFT: **BOLOGNA'S FAMOUS NOBLE TOWERS: A TRIBUTE TO THE FORMER INFLUENCE OF WEALTHY FAMILIES.** *ABOVE*: **THE NEPTUNE FOUNTAIN FROM THE SIXTEENTH CENTURY IS LOCATED ON THE PIAZZA DEL NETTUNO.**

apsed chapel. The same place also houses one of the masterpieces of medieval Italy, the Arca di San Domenico, created by Arnolfo di Cambio. It is an urn embellished with the life story of the church's patron saint.

CONFLICT OF INTERESTS

Bologna has always been a city of both sciences and religion—and both have always been in constant competition. This intellectual conflict—constantly advancing research in sciences, with the church insisting on its dogmas—was especially pronounced in the high Middle Ages. The church tried to convince the people that only faith mattered by building magnificent places of worship. This is the backdrop for the construction of San Francesco. Built in the thirteenth century, it has undergone various alterations but has since been restored to its original appearance. The church ensemble, embellished with many works of art, includes three cloisters.

Although San Petronio is considered Bologna's main church, the city's true cathedral is the so-called Metropolitana, the Cattedrale Metropolitana di San Pietro. The baroque building dating from 1605 invites visitors to admire Ludovico Carracci's last work of art, *Annunciation*, from 1618.

The neighborhood around the Metropolitana is a particularly charming historical district. The Via Altabella quarter, between the Metropolitana and the Church of San Martino, boasts many medieval buildings, including some lower noble towers that have stood the test of time.

Not far away, the Palazzo Ghisilardi Fava houses the Medieval Civic Museum, a charming medieval museum full of statues and bronzes, including precious gold and ivory works. The Via Galliera leads past the museum, an elegant street lined with palaces dating from the fifteenth to the eighteenth centuries.

A CASE OF ITS OWN: GIORGIO MORANDI

Bologna also has modern and contemporary art on offer. The numerous art galleries in the old town are already proof of that. The MAMbo (the Museum of Modern Art) is the most important address in this respect. It presents the artistic movements of Italy since the 1960s. A whole separate section is dedicated to Bologna's most famous modern artist: Giorgio Morandi, who was born in the city in 1890 and died here in 1964. The internationally renowned painter is one of the protagonists of Italy's art history of the twentieth century. His minimalist still lifes appear immensely meditative, which may be why they seem timeless.

Visitors who are tired from all the sightseeing and strolling and are wanting to relax will have plenty of options in the historical center. The best advice is to simply follow where the many young people are going—Bologna is a university town, after all. This is guaranteed to lead you to a welcoming wine bar or trattoria, where you can eat very well (and at a reasonable price at that). Bologna without food, the locals say, is like Rome without the pope.

TUCKING INTO HISTORY

In a city characterized by gastronomy, there are obviously also history-filled places to eat. The Osteria del Sole opened in 1486 and is considered the oldest Bologna restaurant still in operation. It is very quaint and located in the gastronomic heart of the city. But listen up: although the place is called Osteria ("restaurant"), it is in fact a wine bar. You have to bring your own food. But thanks to the many delicatessens in the immediate vicinity, this shouldn't pose a problem.

LEARN MORE

Bologna: www.bolognawelcome.com
MAMbo: www.mambo-bologna.org
Osteria del Sole: www.osteriadelsole.it

RAVENNA – THE IMPERIAL CITY

ROMAN SPLENDOR IN THE PROVINCE

This city was once the center from which a great empire was ruled—but those who don't know about its glorious past may not even notice traces of it nowadays. Yet, it is not for nothing that the city's grandiose buildings from late antiquity are a UNESCO World Heritage Site.

Emperor Augustus had moored large parts of his military fleet in present-day Ravenna on the Adriatic coast. Hundreds of warships were built here. Ravenna was also where the Roman Empire's impressive history, which had begun in the eighth century BCE, eventually ended. In 476 CE, the Germanic officer Odoacer deposed the last Roman Emperor Romulus Augustulus and appointed himself king of Italy.

THE OSTROGOTHS AND BYZANTINES

In 493 CE, the Ostrogoth Theodoric named Ravenna the capital of his empire, which continued to exist until a decisive defeat against the Byzantine Empire with its capital Byzantium. Theodoric was very appreciative of art and was responsible for Ravenna's impressive buildings, which are still unparalleled in Italy.

The religious center of Theodoric's empire was San Vitale. Consecrated in 548 CE, the huge basilica features an octagonal, domed nave at its center. The dome is supported by eight load-bearing pillars and has a diameter of almost 53 feet (16 meters). The church, like many buildings in Ravenna, has been so well preserved because it was built from bricks, according to the tried and tested style of antiquity.

OPPOSITE: THE FORMER PAGAN BAR DANCER THEODORA IS VENERATED IN THIS CHURCH AS A PIOUS EMPRESS. *THIS PAGE:* PURE, UNADULTERATED LATE ANTIQUE ARCHITECTURE—UNIQUE IN ALL OF ITALY.

FANTASTIC MOSAICS

San Vitale is famous for its beautiful and colorful mosaics. Wall and floor mosaics cover almost the entire interior. They illustrate stories from the Old and New Testaments, the Gospels, and the life of Saint Vitalis. They also feature magnificent depictions of Emperor Justinian and his wife, Theodora, one of the most controversial women of her time, as the emperor is said to have met her in a disreputable establishment. What further makes this mosaic fascinating is its portrayal of members of the imperial court, all of whom are dressed in precious garments.

Around 425 CE, a mausoleum was erected right next to San Vitale, dedicated to former Roman Emperor Theodosius I's daughter, Empress Galla Placidia; it might not look very exhilarating from the outside, but it is breathtakingly beautiful inside. However, Galla Placidia actually died in Rome in 450 CE and was probably also buried there and not in Ravenna. The preserved alabaster windows from late antiquity douse the ornate mosaics covering the entire interior in soft light. The mausoleum's ceiling replicates a deep blue sky dotted with white and gold stars. Also featured are the apostles and a young Jesus, still without a beard, portrayed as a good shepherd amidst his flock of sheep.

After a short walk through the rather less spectacular city center of Ravenna, you reach Sant'Apollinare Nuovo from the sixth century. As Theodoric's palace church, it was initially

LEFT: **THE MAUSOLEUM'S DOME WAS CARVED FROM A SINGLE BLOCK OF STONE.**
ABOVE: **IT IS NOT PAINTINGS THAT DECORATE THE NAVE BUT MOSAICS FROM LATE ANTIQUITY.**

consecrated in the Arian faith, a theological doctrine within early Christianity. Yet again, the rather plain and unspectacular exterior is in stark contrast with the magnificent interior, measuring 69 feet (21 meters) wide and 115 feet (35 meters) long. The high central nave is flanked by two lower aisles, separated by ancient columns. The lateral walls of the central nave above the row of columns are entirely covered with ornate mosaics.

The southern wall features a procession of twenty-six saints, led by Saint Martin. In the style of Roman antiquity, the men are dressed in white tunics. The overall impression of these wall mosaics is simply breathtaking. The opposite nave wall is devoted to twenty-two virgins who had lost their lives as martyrs. They are wearing gold-embroidered tunics and white veils. The women are guided by the Three Magi from the Orient. The former mosaics, depicting Theodoric and his entourage, were removed after 540 CE, when the Byzantine Empire conquered Ravenna.

A DECAGONAL TOMB

The Mausoleum of Theodoric, one of the most bizarre in Italy, is considered the most interesting Ostrogoth building in Italy. The monumental tomb is a decagon. Each of the ten walls has a length of 14.4 feet (4.4 meters) and extends over two stories. The roof consists of a shallow dome with a diameter of 36 feet (11 meters). It is 3 feet (1 meter) thick, 8 feet (2.5 meters) high, and weighs approximately 250 tons—and it was carved from a single block of stone. The plain interior exudes a very classical elegance.

The Baptistery of Neon dates back to the fifth century and is also completely intact. It bears the name of Bishop Neon. The mosaics in the dome date from his time and depict saints and evangelists, as well as the typical Ravenna flower decorations that wind around the windows' lunettes.

AN IVORY THRONE

It goes without saying that the two most important museums of Ravenna, the National and the Archiepiscopal Museums, exhibit masterpieces from the era of the Ostrogoths and the Byzantines. The Archiepiscopal Museum houses a special work of art: the throne of Archbishop Maximian from the sixth century—a unique work of ivory carving!

The CLASSIS Museum, which has only been in existence for a handful of years, employs countless

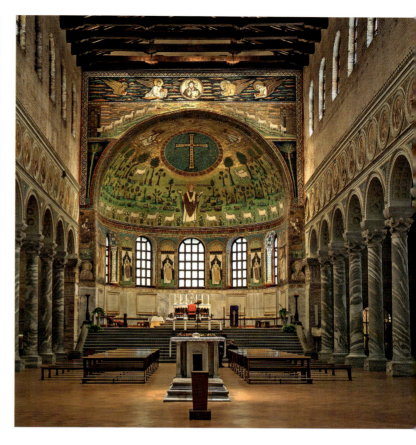

A TREASURE ON A GREEN MEADOW

Three miles (5 kilometers) south of Ravenna, visitors will encounter an architectural treasure. The early Christian church of Sant'Apollinare in Classe was erected where the ancient Romans built their battleships, and it dates back to 549 CE. Its huge interior exhibits precious mosaics from the sixth and seventh centuries—an enormous comic strip from late antiquity featuring saints, prophets, and other characters from the Bible. These mosaics, too, have miraculously withstood the test of time. This magnificent church, however, was not erected by a bishop but built by the late antique banker Giuliano Argentario. Especially beautiful is the apse mosaic featuring Christ as a shepherd standing on a green meadow, surrounded by true-to-life trees under a golden firmament.

LEARN MORE
Ravenna: www.turismo.ra.it
CLASSIS: www.classisravenna.it

archaeological finds to relate the over 2,000 years of Ravenna's history.

Dante's tomb is a more recent addition. Italy's preeminent poet Dante Alighieri died in Ravenna in 1321. His sarcophagus is housed in a building dating from 1780 and marks the goal of a literary pilgrimage for many an Italian.

TRIORA – A VILLAGE IDYLL IN LIGURIA'S MOUNTAINS

SOME DARKNESS AND A LOT OF LIGHT

In the middle of the wooded mountains of the region of Liguria, hidden away and hardly exploited by tourism, are picturesque little villages that seem like they are from a different era. Triora is unquestionably one of the most beautiful mountain villages in Liguria.

Visiting, in the twenty-first century, the romantic village of Triora, surrounded by mountains, forests, and valleys, you would not suspect it possible that a few dozen girls and women of all ages were tried here as witches and burned alive. These shocking events mainly took place in the sixteenth century—a time when humanistic artists in Rome and Florence already heralded a new era. These developments, however, had not yet reached remote Triora. It was as if people were still living in the Middle Ages, and every woman who differed from standard behavior had to fear for her life.

Today, Triora is a picturesque village counting just under four hundred inhabitants, with a downward trend. Situated in the province of Imperia, at an elevation of over 2,500 feet (almost 800 meters), it is located in the hinterland of San Remo, high above the valley of the Argentina River. According to surveys conducted among Italians, Triora is one of the most beautiful villages in the whole country.

It boasts many sites. The remains of five fortresses and castles prove the village's importance in earlier centuries. Four wells once supplied the population with fresh water. A medieval atmosphere dominates here, and you have to be willing to climb to explore Triora. Alleyways and small squares alternate with intimate courtyards, steps, and narrow stairs. Cars are not much use here. The houses are nestled side by side, and only the darkest of alleys give a hint of Triora once being a site of horror for its inhabitants.

OPPOSITE: **TRIORA IS PERCHED ON A HILL AMID A WILD MOUNTAIN LANDSCAPE.**
LEFT: **THIS MOUNTAIN VILLAGE SEEMS ESPECIALLY ROMANTIC AND MYSTERIOUS AFTER NIGHTFALL.**

A DARK PAST...

Numerous women and girls became the victims of the Catholic Church's ruthless inquisition—huge swaths, given how small the Italian village is. These women were accused of everything that could not be rationally explained, ranging from diseases to failed harvests, from the plague to the inexplicable deaths of domestic and farm animals. An anonymous accusation was enough to bring a victim before an Inquisition judge. The village's chronicles feature many horrific stories of presumed witches.

The worst year was 1587. After a dramatic famine caused by bad weather, a majority of citizens were convinced it was the work of witches. Initially, twenty women were on trial, then thirty. The inquisitor, sent from Genoa, attested to their "guilt." Most of the women died in the flames.

Nowadays, the witch hunt past has become a lucrative source of income. Quaint stores sell handmade witch dolls. The story of the witches of Triora is retold in the only Italian witches' museum, the Museo della Stregoneria.

...AND A CHEERFUL PRESENT

Take your time for a stroll through Triora and plan on spending the night in a local accommodation. The place offers such a relaxing atmosphere that one can barely believe that the bustling Italian Riviera is only an hour's drive away.

Both churches in Triora are worth a visit. The Collegiata dell'Assunta, with its Romanesque and Gothic roots, displays wooden carvings by Taddeo di Bartolo and Luca Cambiaso. The baptistry, the building with the baptismal font, dates from the baroque era. The Church of San Bernardino, built in the fifteenth century, features a fresco cycle by Ligurian-Piedmontese painters.

CULINARY DISCOVERIES

If you come to Triora in August or September, you have the chance to taste all kinds of delicacies in the various villages in the area, during the so-called "sagre," which are food festivals dedicated to local delicacies. These include the small, punchy Taggiasca olives, as well as "canestrelli," which are pastry rings baked with salt and the local olive oil. Another real specialty is the "stocafaissu di badalucco," stockfish with olive oil, garlic, anchovies, nuts, and pine nuts. Whether it is porcino mushrooms or snails, vegetables or homemade spiced schnapps (according to recipes allegedly handed down from the witches), there is so much to try that Triora and its surrounding area are considered inside tips among gourmets.

LEARN MORE
Triora: www.trioradascoprire.it
Witch Museum/Museo Etnografico e della Stregoneria: www.museotriora.it

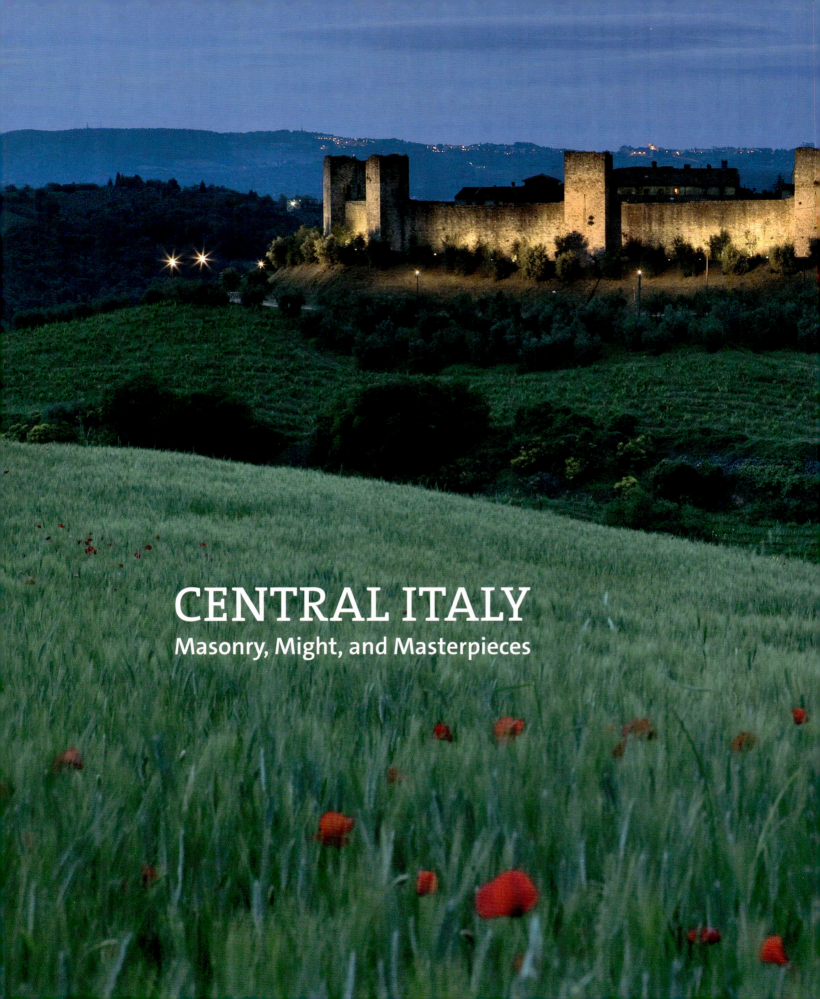

CENTRAL ITALY
Masonry, Might, and Masterpieces

ONE OF MONTERIGGIONI'S CITY GATES POINTS TOWARD FLORENCE, ANOTHER LEADS TO SIENA. APART FROM THAT, A COMPLETE WALL OF 1,870 FEET (570 METERS) ENCIRCLES THE TOWN.

21

ORSIGNA – THE ELECTIVE HOME OF TIZIANO TERZANI
A PLACE FOR THE HEART

For many years, the famous journalist and legendary foreign correspondent, who reported from numerous countries, especially in Asia, felt a pull toward this small and quiet place. Tiziano Terzani also chose to die here.

"Orsigna brought poetry to my life. I keep coming back here since I was a boy; it is the place of my heart and my refuge." Nowhere else did the German-Italian foreign correspondent and travel journalist Tiziano Terzani prefer to spend time than in Orsigna, a village hidden in the mountains at about 2,630 feet (800 meters). Pistoia is located about 19 miles (30 kilometers) south of Orsigna. The village is surrounded by dense forests, and only about sixty people live here. From Florence, the journey takes about an hour by car. Shortly before reaching your destination, the roads get increasingly narrow and curvy. Terzani called the mountains near Orsigna "my Himalayas."

HIKING ON TERZANI'S TRAILS

Terzani died here in July 2004 at the age of only sixty-five years after a long illness. It was here that he wrote his last book, *One More Ride on the Merry-Go-Round* (translated by Felix Bolling), which also immortalizes Orsigna. This shocking and simultaneously encouraging book is a conversation between the cancer-stricken journalist and his son,

Folco. In it, Terzani calls his slow process of dying, which he attentively observes, and his imminent death his "last great adventure."

The town does not have a lot of famous sons and daughters, so it comes as no surprise that Orsigna boasts a 3-mile-long (5 kilometers) trail commemorating the author. Called the Sentiero di Terzani, it takes you from the village to the "Albero con gli occhi"—the "tree with eyes"—a large old tree that Terzani greatly adored.

LONESOME ROUTES

The area around Orsigna has been able to preserve its aura as a secret spot, and it is not alone. The whole region—from the Apennine Mountains west of the Autostrada del Sole leading from Florence to Bologna, to the Apuan Alps between Massa by the sea and the medieval town of Barga—is far from overflowing with tourists. Here you can still find it, the original Tuscany: a lot of untouched nature and villages, which may not boast great art or architecture but show real life, without tourism or serving folklore purposes.

This is probably why Terzani decided to settle in Orsigna at the end of his life. And it is also why at least a few Italian and foreign hikers make their way to the mountains between Orsigna and Massa: to be in nature, to rent holiday homes that are still affordable, and to experience nature that has not been man-made.

AN ALMOST FORGOTTEN HEALTH RESORT

In the nineteenth century, the region was better known thanks to its thermal springs. Nowadays, the spa town Bagni di Lucca is a sleepy little village. It is hard to believe that Julius Caesar and the Renaissance poet Boccaccio have visited the spa, as have Prince Metternich and Heinrich Heine, and

OPPOSITE: **TIZIANO TERZANI GAZES OVER HIS HOME IN THE NORTH OF TUSCANY.** *BELOW*: **ORSIGNA OFFERS TUSCANY IN A WAY THAT FEW VISITORS WILL GET TO SEE IT.**

composers such as Rossini, Verdi, and Puccini. Today, everything in Bagni seems a little like it comes from another, distant time. It's a place with a very special charm.

Extensive forests cover the area between Barga and Orsigna. Narrow alleyways lead through the dense greenery to picturesque villages that are only inhabited by a few people—if they are inhabited at all. About 50 miles (80 kilometers) of roads take you through the most beautiful scenery the wild Tuscany landscape has to offer. Tuscany, as Tiziano Terzani often described it. Many years ago. And it has barely changed since then.

BARGA PLAYS BAROQUE

There is not only an impressive Romanesque cathedral in Barga, but the town is also the location for a privately organized festival of classical music that has been staged here for more than fifty years. Opera Barga puts on at least one baroque opera every year, staged at the late eighteenth-century municipal opera house Teatro dei Differenti, with seats for only 289 spectators. The festival originated with a private initiative and is already being organized in the second generation. It was founded in 1967 by the Brits Peter Hunt and Gillian Armitage together with the German conductor Peter Gellhorn. Most of the baroque operas are new productions of works that have not been performed elsewhere for a long time.

LEARN MORE
Festival Barga: www.operabarga.it

LA VERNA – A PLACE FOR HOLY LEGENDS

CLEAR HEAD AND DEEP CONTEMPLATION

There is always a fresh breeze here—even when high summer exerts an oppressive heat on Umbria. This is probably part of the reason why Francis of Assisi decided to build a monastery on this mountain. He is said to have received the stigmata of Christ on Mount Alverna in 1224.

A place steeped in history. Close to nature. Wild, romantic, and pleasantly cool in the summer. La Verna is located on the southwestern slope of Monte Penna at an altitude of about 3,770 feet (1,150 meters). The village and landscape lead to some of the most important locations in Francis of Assisi's development early on. In 1213, Count Orlando Catani from nearby Chiusi bequeathed the part of the mountain called Monte Alverna to Francis of Assisi and the Order of the Frias Minor, since Francis was already venerated as a saint during his lifetime. But it was only a year later that Francis himself climbed up the mountain.

The present monastery was not built during the saint's lifetime. Initially, only a chapel was erected, the Cappella Santa Maria degli Angeli, and a few spartan huts for the monks. But the place is important for the saint's hagiography because, according to the poet Dante in his *Divine Comedy*, it was here that Francis "received the last seal of Christ," that is, the stigmata.

The basilica of the La Verna monastery was not created until after Francis's death, between the fourteenth and the early sixteenth centuries—in the plain style of the late Middle Ages and a very elegant early Renaissance.

DELICATE TERRACOTTA ART

Among the most precious works of art from this era are fifteen glazed terracotta panels by the Florence artist family della Robbia, who were already famous in their time. They depict scenes from the New

OPPOSITE: **A MONASTERY WITH PANORAMIC VIEWS AMID UNTAMED NATURE.** *LEFT*: **THE ENAMELED TERRACOTTA ART IS ONE OF THE MASTERPIECES OF RENAISSANCE LA VERNA.** *BELOW*: **EXPERIENCING A VERY DEEP SILENCE—IN FRANCIS'S MONASTERY.**

Testament. Andrea della Robbia created one of the most beautiful of these panels in 1476, and it is now displayed in a side chapel.

The wooden choir stalls from 1495 have been preserved as well, as has a lectern for the Scriptures from 1509. The case housing the organ is one of the oldest in Italy, dating from the fifteenth century. The modern 1926 organ it contains has 5,500 pipes. Hearing it sound out is a marvellous experience.

Every altar in the Catholic Church guards a relic, and that of La Verna is no exception. Under the main altar is a coffin with the remains of Giovanni della Verna. He was a revered hermit who lived on the mountain around the turn of the thirteenth to the fourteenth century.

SACRED CAMP

Through a more than 260-foot-long (80 meters) corridor, the Corridor of the Stigmata, visitors and pilgrims reach the Chiesa delle Stimmate, the Chapel of the Stigmata. At the center of this "corridor" is a cave that is always cool and uncomfortably damp. It is called the "bed of St. Francis" and dates back to the 1260s. This cave features a particularly beautiful terracotta panel by Andrea della Robbia; it depicts a large-scale crucifixion scene with mourning angels.

The small church of Santa Maria degli Angeli is said to have been built at exactly the spot where, according to pious legend, the Blessed Mother appeared to Francis of Assisi. It is said that Mary gave the monk precise instructions as to where and how to build the first church on the mountain. This Chiesina, the chapel, was built between 1216 and 1218 and expanded later on. Andrea and Giovanni della Robbia also immortalized themselves here with terracotta reliefs. The simple Franciscan monastery La Verna has cloisters dating from the fourteenth century. The refectory measures a staggering 128 feet (39 meters). The region is also ideal for walkers—the monastery forms the perfect starting point for a hike.

SILENT NIGHTS

If you like solitude, the monastery's Foresteria—its guesthouse—is the ideal place to stay. It offers guest rooms with simple comforts, not only for pious pilgrims but also for hikers. Simple but hearty dishes according to Umbrian tradition are served in the pilgrims' dining room. Fruit and vegetables are partly sourced from the monastery's own garden, and the wine comes from the immediate surroundings. If you would like to delve even deeper into contemplation, you can ask for a space for silence and prayer right here in the monastery, where the monks live and tourists have no access. All those are allowed to stay in the monastery who adhere to the rules. In the Casa di Preghiera, the house of prayer, everyone receives an introduction to the Franciscans' way of life.

LEARN MORE
La Verna: www.laverna.it

THIS PAGE: A PALACE? A CASTLE? A WHOLE TOWN? URBINO'S DUCAL PALACE IS ONE OF THE MOST BEAUTIFUL IN CENTRAL ITALY. *OPPOSITE*: THE MOST IMPORTANT INTELLECTUALS OF THEIR TIME TAUGHT IN THE PALAZZO DUCALE AND WERE PAINTED BY THE MOST FAMOUS ARTISTS.

URBINO – TREASURE TROVE IN THE MARCHES

TREASURES BEHIND THE SCENES

Urbino, in the Marche region, offers a walled old town that can be easily explored in an hour. The elegant historical façades conceal an abundance of Renaissance treasures, which make it worth considering a longer stay.

It may be difficult to believe, but Urbino was once a capital city. The House of Montefeltro ruled their small duchy from here. The family's heyday was in the Renaissance—and it seems today as if the small town somehow got stuck in that era. The historic town center—with its picturesque streets and squares, its churches, and its palaces—looks like a nearly perfect set for a movie that takes place in the fifteenth and sixteenth centuries.

WARRIOR AND ART CONNOISSEUR

One of the dukes in particular, Federico da Montefeltro, devoted himself to fine arts. It was his passion and expertise that transformed little Urbino into a big city of the arts. To this day, it is a popular destination for art lovers—who never even get in the way of each other, since Urbino lies far off the beaten tourist path. Federico was successful as a condottiere (a military leader) and came into great wealth. He invested a great deal of his income from the business of war into culture. His court was famous throughout Italy. He managed to attract important artists to his mini-state, such as Piero della Francesca, the painter and sculptor Francesco di Giorgio Martini, and Raphael's father, Giovanni Santi, who facilitated an artists' workshop in Urbino until his death.

ROYAL SEAT AND MUSEUM

The largest and most important historical building of Urbino is the Ducal Palace. It is considered the archetype of a fortified royal residence of the Italian Renaissance. The mighty building was chosen as the home of the Galleria Nazionale delle Marche, the National Gallery of Art, which displays the most important works of the Marches region. It is undoubtedly one of the most important museums in Central Italy. And that is saying something, in Italy, a country bursting with art!

The historical halls of the da Montefeltro family have great things in store for visitors: there are stately apartments with magnificent series of rooms and some chambers that also reflect the owner Federico's intellectual interests. The Palazzetto della Jole occupies a complete wing of the majestic ducal seat.

A CABINET FOR CONTEMPLATION AND CURIOSITIES

There is, for example, the so-called "studiolo," a special kind of study. It's a small room of about 13 by 10 feet (4 by 3 meters) in size, and the walls are decorated with wood inlay works. Their trompe-l'œil effect makes the observer see landscapes, buildings, and gardens on the walls. This inlay craft also represents the liberal arts, musical instruments and scores, books, and scientific tools, as well as the types of items that princes back then would collect in their cabinets of curiosities. The studiolo is a space unlike any other in Italy.

LEFT: **URBINO'S MAIN ROAD IS THE LIVELY CENTER OF THIS SMALL TOWN.** *ABOVE:* **LATE GOTHIC MURALS EMBELLISH THE ORATORY OF SAN GIOVANNI BATTISTA.**

The da Montefeltro family were people of the Renaissance, through and through. This means that they presented themselves as practicing Catholics but also glorified anything originating in antiquity. The twin chapels illustrate this particularly well: one of them is dedicated to the muses—that is, to the arts; the other to God. In Federico da Montefeltro's days, some members of the cleric already considered these chapels a sacrilege.

Almost the entire palace is nowadays a museum. The paintings on display here are simply stunning: main works by Titian, Paolo Uccello, Melozzo da Forlì, Luca della Robbia, Botticelli, Bramantino, and many others. Reserve at least half a day for a relaxing tour of this museum. The ever-changing views from the many windows out onto the lush green surroundings of Urbino and the historical sea of city roofs are also very attractive.

One of the most remarkable sacred buildings of Urbino is San Giovanni Battista. The oratory is a work of the thirteenth century. The plain interior hides a genuine fresco treasure: a cycle of murals recounting the life of St. John and the crucifixion, painted in 1418 by the brothers Jacopo and Lorenzo Salimbeni.

VISITING RAPHAEL

The cathedral, on the other hand, is a bit of a disappointment. It was commissioned by Federico da Montefeltro. After an earthquake in 1789, Giuseppe Valadier, one of the most famous architects and designers of his time, was entrusted with the reconstruction of this neoclassical church. The design looks quite cold and has little in common with Urbino's Renaissance atmosphere. Through a door on the right-hand side of the nave, inside the cathedral, visitors reach the Museo Albani. This small but exclusive collection includes medieval murals, ceramics, and elaborately embroidered clerical garments from various centuries. It also boasts important paintings, including *The Last Supper* by Federico Barocci. Barocci is considered one of the most important painters of the period between the Renaissance and the baroque eras.

Urbino is also the birthplace of Raphael, one of the greatest Renaissance artists, yet he only created a single piece in his hometown. Probably because his father, a painter, died when Raphael was still a child. His son pursued his career further afield. Raphael's birthplace, the Casa Natale di Raffaello, is still intact and open to visitors. It is located on—of course—the Via Raffaello. The curators have tried their best to create an authentic atmosphere using historical furniture, copies of Raphael's works, and original paintings by his father.

SAN LEO – A FORTRESS FOR A WOMANIZER
Less than a thirty-minute drive north of Urbino, the fortress of San Leo towers on a spur nearly 2,000 feet (600 meters) over the landscape. The fort from the tenth century (converted and expanded in the fifteenth) resisted conquest for a long time and is now one of the most beautiful and best-preserved fortresses in Italy. A small museum displays Renaissance paintings and offers a fantastic panorama all the way to the Adriatic coast. San Leo, which was used as a prison of the Papal States in the eighteenth century, was the place where one of the then most famous crooks of his time served his sentence. Originally from Palermo, Giuseppe Balsamo committed his monstrous deeds all over Europe under the alias Count Cagliostro. As a womanizer, swindler, thief, alchemist, and blasphemer, he was sentenced to life in prison. Cagliostro only survived the harsh conditions of solitary confinement for four years.

Learn More
Urbino: www.vieniaurbino.it
Ducal Palace: www.gallerianazionalemarche.it

24

MONTERIGGIONI – THE ROUND MIRACLE
CROWNED WITH TOWERS

It towers on the hill, an almost perfect circle: the walls of this marvelous Tuscan village can be seen from afar. A place that has barely changed since the time of Dante, who immortalized it in his *Divine Comedy*.

Upon visiting Monteriggioni, many visitors wonder why they don't just buy a cottage here. Here, where Tuscany, already rich in magical places, emits a very special kind of charm. Monteriggioni is unique in Tuscany. You will notice this when you approach the village by car. The mighty walls can be spotted from far away, forming a near-perfect fortified circle.

DANTE'S MONTERIGGIONI
This is what the poet once observed:

> *for as, on its round wall, Montereggioni*
> *is crowned with towers, so there towered here,*
> *above the bank that runs around the pit,*
> *with half their bulk, the terrifying giants,*
> *whom Jove still menaces from Heaven when*
> *he sends his bolts of thunder down upon them.*

Dante Alighieri used these words, famous in Italy, to describe Monteriggioni in the *Inferno* section of his *Divine Comedy*.

This plain village, situated on a hill at a height of 656 feet (200 meters), was founded in the thirteenth century as a defensive base of the Republic of Siena—independent from Florence back then—hence the elaborate system of walls and fortified towers. It is the first new construction of a town wall without an accompanying castle in

OPPOSITE: **NOT MUCH HAS CHANGED IN MONTERIGGIONI SINCE THE MIDDLE AGES—FORTUNATELY!** LEFT: **A BREAK IN THIS VILLAGE IS THE EQUIVALENT OF TOTAL RELAXATION, WITHOUT ANY HYPE OR HUBBUB.**

Tuscany; up until then, only existing castles were equipped with such an impressive defense system. The town's name either comes from the Latin Montis Regis, "royal mountain," or Mons Regionis, the region's "highest mountain."

RECORD-BREAKING WALL

This wall ring is 1,870 feet (570 meters) long, with walls 6.6 feet (2 meters) thick and fourteen mighty perimeter towers. A defensive corridor leads all the way around. Each of the towers is 20 by 13 feet (6 by 4 meters) and 49 feet (15 meters) tall. At around 574 feet (175 meters), the diameter of the defense system covers the entire surface of the hill. Entry into the fortified town is still accessed through one of two gates. The lower gate, the Porta di Sotto, was built in the direction of Florence, while the Porta Franca, also known as Porta Romea, points towards Rome. Behind the walls lies the village—picturesque, mostly deserted, and very quiet. There are no buildings of art history interest in this village, yet a very harmonious ensemble of perfectly restored houses await visitors.

Monteriggioni's main church, Santa Maria Assunta, dates back to the thirteenth century. The monastery church San Rocco is built in the baroque style of the eighteenth century. A couple of charming places of worship are located just outside the village, such as San Lorenzo a Colle Ciupi in the Località Riciano. The medieval church is adorned with a fresco of the Madonna, children, and saints—a piece from the workshop of the Gothic painter Duccio di Buoninsegna, a respected master of his time.

IMMORTALIZED IN NUMEROUS MOVIES

The main square of Monteriggioni and its narrow alleys have repeatedly featured in movies. Franco Zeffirelli, Ridley Scott, Bernardo Bertolucci, Mario Monicelli, and others have shot scenes in this romantic place.

It is a special treat to stay overnight in Monteriggioni. When the few tourists have left, the village becomes even more tranquil. You feel like you are transported to a different era. Sitting in the piazza in the evening, enjoying perfect peace and quiet in this special atmosphere while sipping a glass of wine—what seems like a cliché of idyllic Tuscan life comes true in Monteriggioni.

PERFECT HIKING CONDITIONS

Take a few days to visit Monteriggioni and its immediate surroundings. There are charming hiking trails and bicycle paths to old monasteries and Renaissance palaces, lonesome lakes, and woods in this area. Monteriggioni's tourist office has all the important information you need, in Italian and English. The well-sign-posted trails are mostly easy going and perfect for a day hike. The locals have used these paths since Dante's time—that is, for centuries.

LEARN MORE
Monteriggioni: www.monteriggioniturismo.it

THIS PAGE: **GUBBIO IN A PARTY MOOD:** ON MAY 15, THE CORSA DEI CERI PARADE CULMINATES IN THE MAIN SQUARE. *OPPOSITE:* THE REST OF THE YEAR, THIS IS A RATHER QUIET TOWN.

GUBBIO – STROLLING THROUGH THE MIDDLE AGES
UMBRIA'S BALCONY

The small town, with its medieval center, extends up a mountain slope. Like in an amphitheater, the houses climb up, one after the other. From its palaces, churches, and squares, visitors have magnificent views of the surrounding countryside.

Even the pre-Roman people of the region, the Umbri, appreciated the prime location. At an elevation of 1,738 feet (530 meters), Gubbio always has a refreshing breeze. The ancient town of Iguvium must have been pretty wealthy; it even coined its own currency. The so-called Iguvine Tablets also date from this period, the third century BCE. They constitute the oldest bronze tablets in the Umbrian language.

The Romans were followed by the Byzantines. Gubbio was situated on the road between Rome and Ravenna, the emperor's seat, and benefited economically from this location. It goes without saying that the town quickly gained influence in the Middle Ages. From the twelfth to the fourteenth centuries, it was politically independent. Then, it belonged to the Duchy of Urbino; later, in the early seventeenth century, Gubbio fell to the Papal States, which resulted in a long period of political, economic, and cultural stagnation. That stagnation, however, is why the medieval city center has been preserved.

GUBBIO'S RECEPTION ROOM
The Piazza della Signoria, or simply Piazza Grande, "the great square," is the center of Gubbio. It's a

rectangular square with fantastic views of the beautiful surrounding landscape. Two mighty palaces tower over the piazza. The Palazzo Pretorio, with its severe and somewhat hostile façade, now serves as the town hall. Built in the fourteenth century, there are three halls on top of each other inside, covered by impressive vaulted ceilings.

Directly opposite is the Palazzo dei Consoli, one of the most beautiful examples of secular medieval architecture. This elegant building made of large stone blocks is crowned by a slender tower. This building, too, dates back to the fourteenth century, Gubbio's architectural heyday. The architect, Angelo da Orvieto, confidently immortalized himself by engraving his own name above the main entrance—which was a rarity at that time.

The palace's ground floor consists of a single, large room. This was where council and citizens' meetings took place. The floor above houses a small but exquisite Pinacoteca comunale. The municipal art collection, arranged in the original halls of the representative building, displays the seven famous bronze plates of the Umbri as well as Etruscan and Roman finds from the surrounding area. The paintings from the late Middle Ages to the baroque period are particularly beautiful as well.

SMALL DISCOVERIES

It is very charming to simply float through the alleys of this village. Strollers will encounter small cafés and pleasant bars, delicatessens offering local specialties, and arts and crafts stores, as well as a fairly uniform architectural vibe. For example, on the Via dei Consoli, many of the medieval houses feature a so-called "porta del morto," a "door of the dead." The gates above street level were allegedly only added to carry deceased people out of the houses. The Via Baldassini also boasts residential buildings from the thirteenth and fourteenth centuries. By following the picturesque streets Via Vantaggi and Via Gabrielli, you will reach the Palazzo del Capitano del Popolo, which is one of Gubbio's most beautiful buildings and dates back to the fifteenth century.

NOT AT ALL A VOW OF POVERTY

The church San Francesco also dates from the thirteenth century. Behind the simple façade, with its Romanesque portal, lies a church with a central nave, two aisles, and several side altars. A cycle of frescoes by the local painter Ottaviano Nelli from the fifteenth century recounts the life of Mary, Mother of God. Further murals date from the thirteenth and fourteenth centuries. The church treasure proves that the clergy of San Francesco did not take their Franciscan vow of poverty entirely seriously; it comprises precious gold work and richly embroidered robes. The Gothic cathedral rises at the highest point of Gubbio. You will reach

THE CANDLE RACE
Come to Gubbio on May 15! That is when a most curious procession takes place. At the annual Corsa dei Ceri, the so-called candle race—in honor of the town's patron saint, Saint Ubald of Gubbio—three teams compete in different colors. Each team carries a 16-foot-tall (5 meters) statute, weighing 882 pounds (400 kilograms). One statue represents Ubald; the second, St. Anthony; and the third, St. George. Though, from the very beginning, it is clear who will win the race through the streets—as per tradition, the patron saint! The other two teams have to run more slowly. Almost the entire population takes part in the most important folk festival of the year.

LEARN MORE
Gubbio: www.umbriaturismo.net
Palazzo dei Consoli: www.palazzodeiconsoli.it

it after a nice walk through the narrow alleyways. The church was built on the foundations of a former Romanesque place of worship and includes some of the sculptures of its predecessor.

CATHEDRAL AT AN ANGLE

You will instantly feel that this church was built on a slope. Not only does the square in front of the cathedral have a steep incline, but parts of its interior do as well. The single nave features sturdy flying buttresses that stabilize the entire building. It houses important works of religious art, such as a Madonna with the dead Son of God, a pietà by Dono Doni from the sixteenth century, and an artfully crafted Nativity scene from the workshop of painter Pinturicchio, dating to the late fifteenth century. The intricately carved choir stalls were crafted in the sixteenth century, as was the bishop's throne, which is still in use today.

The cathedral's treasure also includes frescoes and gold works as well as gorgeous, well-preserved clerical robes lavishly embroidered in silver and gold. The Ducal Palace is located by the cathedral. Built in the late fifteenth century by Duke Federico da Montefeltro, this building surprises with a beautiful courtyard from the Renaissance period.

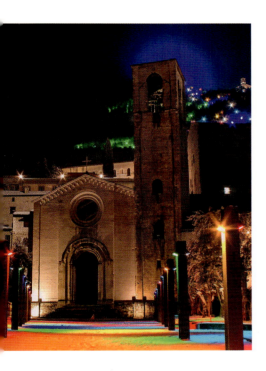

ABOVE: **ON THE OUTSIDE, GUBBIO'S CATHEDRAL LOOKS RATHER PLAIN.**
RIGHT: **THE ENTIRE INTERIOR, HOWEVER, IS DECORATED WITH PAINTINGS FROM SEVERAL CENTURIES.**

SAN GALGANO – MYSTERIOUS MIDDLE AGES

A CHURCH ASPIRING TO HEAVEN

What a ruin! Anyone who claims that dreamy church ruins are the prerogative of England will find out that they are wrong. San Galgano is one of the most romantic and mysterious places in Italy. You should take your time exploring it, step by step.

The village of San Galgano is located about 22 miles (35 kilometers) southwest of Siena. You can get there by car—but then you should park somewhere and approach the ruins on foot. If you follow this advice, you will see a mighty building rise from nature, from the forests and fields around you. There is no trace of modern buildings—just the ruin and almost nothing else.

This impressive set of walls, where the wind whistles through the windows and where the sun shines straight in (because there is no roof), used to be a wealthy Cistercian abbey.

FROM WARRIOR TO SAINT

In 1185, the Bishop of Volterra decided to have a church built at the spot where Saint Galgano was said to have died. Galgano Guidotti spent a big part of his life as a knight. After divine inspiration struck, however, he decided to live as a hermit.

Construction began in 1218. The money for the impressive abbey church was donated by wealthy Tuscan nobility, and the architecture was inspired by monks of Clairvaux Abbey in France. The monastery quickly prospered, partly because the monks drained the swamps and trained themselves to become masters of agriculture.

Yet famines and plague epidemics beginning in the fourteenth century led to the economic decline of the monastery. During the war between Siena and Florence, the abbey was attacked by the Florentines in 1364. In 1783, the Austrian Grand Duke of Tuscany, Leopold I, dissolved the monastery. The bell tower collapsed, then the roof and the other buildings, one after the other. In the meantime, farmers inhabited the complex. From the 1960s onwards, the Cistercians returned and now manage the ruin.

OPPOSITE: AFTER NIGHTFALL, SAN GALGANO PRESENTS ITSELF PERFECTLY ILLUMINATED. *LEFT*: CYPRESS TREES LINE THE AVENUE LEADING TO THE PICTURESQUE MONASTERY RUIN.

A LA FRANÇAISE

The church is 233 feet (71 meters) long and 69 feet (21 meters) wide. This is the first ever example of Gothic architecture anywhere in Tuscany. Yet, the northern European style never really took off in Italy. The church, with its nave and two aisles, is modeled on the form of a Latin cross. Elegant, slender columns with capitals protrude into the air, into the space where the roof once was. The cloisters and the impressive chapter house have remained partially intact. The style of the monastery complex is reminiscent of French edifices, such as those in Burgundy. In Italy, this is a rarity.

SWORD IN THE STONE

Opposite the ruins is a circular Romanesque church on a hill. The two-tone church interior houses a rock. In it is the sword of a medieval knight. Galgano Guidotti is said to have driven this lethal weapon into the stone as a sign of peace.

It is worth visiting the small church and the ruined abbey in bad weather, at sunrise or sunset—when the place is almost deserted and, as is frequently the case, wafts of mist seem to disguise the ruins and the other buildings. In this atmosphere, the location takes on a mystical aura and looks almost out of place in the middle of the charming Tuscany landscape. The famous Russian director Andrei Tarkovsky must have had the same feeling, because the impressive closing sequence of his 1983 movie *Nostalghia* shows the ruined abbey at its finest. It is thanks to this movie that San Galgano became known to a wider audience.

ANCIENT HEALTH SPA

The Roman politician and author Cicero is said to have bathed in the open-air natural basins of Terme di Petriolo, about 19 miles (30 kilometers) southeast of San Galgano—probably to recover from the stresses of Roman life back then by splashing about in the warm springs of 109 degrees Fahrenheit (43 degrees Celsius). The first thermal spa complex was built here during the Renaissance. Even Renaissance Pope Pius II allegedly cleansed his respiratory tract here. The limescale deposits that have formed on the rocks since ancient times are very impressive. A plunge in the natural baths is free of charge. You can stay over in the nearby village of Monticiano and enjoy a fantastic Tuscan meal.

LEARN MORE

Abbey of San Galgano: www.comune.chiusdino.siena.it
Terme di Petriolo: www.termepetriolo.it

GIARDINO SPOERRI – A GARDEN FULL OF IDEAS
ART WHEREVER YOU GO

Stroll through a park with artsy surprises around every bush and tree—and with German phrases that can be read forwards and backwards. Swiss artist Daniel Spoerri created his very own modern art paradise in the countryside near Seggiano.

"Gin ohne banknoten – essen etonknaben honig," "leo zieh heizoel," and "essölklösse": these enigmatic German words and phrases greet visitors upon entering the art garden. They are so-called palindromes—letter compositions that can be read from front to back and vice versa. The artist André Thomkins created them for his friend and Swiss artist peer, former dancer and director Daniel Spoerri.

ARTISTIC DOMICILE IN TUSCANY
Spoerri, a native Romanian and naturalized Swiss, initially worked as a dancer before becoming a painter and installation artist living variously in Zurich, New York, Paris, and Germany, until he eventually settled in the Tuscan town of Seggiano. In the 1990s, he acquired a rural estate and made it his home and studio space.

But Spoerri didn't just want to put his feet up and sit in the Tuscan sun, creating a little art here and there. His goal was to bring nature and art together, and his idea met with approval from his many artist friends.

Visitors will discover dozens of works of art on 40 acres (16 hectares) of land that has been only partially landscaped and tamed—everything seems a little wild and untrimmed. Sturdy footwear is needed because after rainfall, it can be damp and muddy underfoot.

OPPOSITE: **CONTEMPORARY ART AT SUNSET: SPOERRI'S SCULPTURE PARK OFFERS SURPRISES AT ANY TIME OF THE DAY.** *LEFT*: **WORKS BY THE MASTER HIMSELF AND HIS ARTIST FRIENDS ARE OFTEN HIDDEN AMONG THE NATURE OF HIS ART GARDEN.**

SCULPTURES OF ANY KIND

The works are placed seemingly indiscriminately in the greenery. While there is, of course, a map to show visitors how to get to each installation, it is just as appealing to just go explore and let yourself be surprised. About fifty sculptures are by Daniel Spoerri himself, with an additional one hundred by his friends. Among them are some big names from the more recent art scene, such as Eva Aeppli, Alfonso Hüppi, Nam June Paik, Jean Tinguely, and Roland Topor.

Again and again, artists created land art, some of which is rather huge. Swiss artist and sculptor Olivier Estoppey called his piece *Day of Wrath*; it's a herd of fantastical four-legged animals. There's also the installation *Fertile Earth* by Italian Luigi Mainolfi, which features high iron towers topped with terracotta tips. Turin artist Aldo Mondino designed *Grande Arabesque*, a fish balancing on one leg. In the shade of the trees, German artist Uwe Schloen built 6-foot-tall buildings made of wood and lead. His *Bunker Village* seems strange at first glance, but when you look closer, it almost harmoniously blends into the landscape.

NATURE AND ART IN HARMONY

Daniel Spoerri's *Unicorns* point into the Tuscan sky as if they had become a natural part of the gentle landscape. The master of the house erected his sculpture—a circle with the horns of mythological unicorns—at the edge of the garden, where you can enjoy a magnificent view of the open landscape. Sunsets here are simply breathtaking.

If you find it difficult to leave the sculpture garden, you can spend the night. The owner has set up a few vacation apartments in the main house, which are large and comfortably furnished. When the park closes at dusk, you get to live in the middle of a composition of art and nature.

ABBEY OF SANT'ANTIMO – A BLESSED PLACE

Set in the countryside, eighth-century Benedictine monks created this beautiful Romanesque abbey church in a particularly remote place. The severe features of the Cistercian style dominate the architecture. The abbey's clear, elegant lines require no additional embellishments. Only the imaginative capitals atop the pillars are richly adorned with saints, monsters, hybrid creatures that are half animal and half human, and scenes from the Bible. The main nave extends over two stories and is subdivided by archways. The apse dates to the eighth century, when the Carolingians reigned over Europe. The campanile is embellished with a delicate relief of the Madonna and the Evangelists, a strict composition from the twelfth century.

LEARN MORE
Il Giardino di Daniel Spoerri: www.danielspoerri.org
Abbazia di Sant'Antimo: www.antimo.it

THE PICTURESQUE VILLAGE OF SEGGIANO IS LOCATED AMONG THE HILLY LANDSCAPE OF SOUTHERN TUSCANY.

THIS PAGE: **LA DOLCE VITA: SITTING IN THE BAR TRIC TRAC AND RELAXING ON THE PIAZZA BY THE CATHEDRAL.** *OPPOSITE:* **A MAGNIFICENT VIEW OF THE MEDIEVAL AQUEDUCT WITH THE FORTRESS OF SPOLETO.**

SPOLETO – A FESTIVAL MAKES HISTORY
SUDDENLY FAMOUS

Spoleto is in a very picturesque location on a slope above romantic valleys. Suddenly famous in the 1950s after years of stagnation, this very special spot is one of Italy's most culturally active small towns.

In 1957, the Italian composer Gian Carlo Menotti, who lived in the US at the time, traveled to Umbria. He was looking for a small town with several theaters. In his elective home country, Menotti was considered one of the most important contemporary composers, so he wanted to give back some of his success to his home country—in the form of art: a festival.

A CELEBRITY HUB
Menotti found what he was after in the sleepy town of Spoleto. It was a beautiful and charming place with architectural appeal, complete with various squares and palaces, churches, and proud townhouses, perched on a hill with a castle on the top. And it already entertained three theaters: a small one, Caio Melisso, on the cathedral square, which was founded in the seventeenth century; an opera house from the nineteenth century; and a Roman amphitheater in the middle of the old town.

The town offered perfect conditions for a cultural event. The composer founded the Festival dei Due Mondi, which took place for the first time in 1958. Since Menotti was a man with great connections to the financial world, he did not have to contend with economic hurdles at the get-go. Spoleto became one of the most important places in Italy for opera, theater, dance, and fine arts—almost overnight.

Menotti managed to bring the most important names of his time to Spoleto, including writers such as Tennessee Williams, choreographers such as Jerome Robbins, directors such as Luchino Visconti, singers such as Luciano Pavarotti, and sculptors such as Alexander Calder. Following these cultural celebrities, the international jet set also came to Spoleto. The two-week summer festival was the cultural highlight of the Italian events calendar until Menotti's death in 2007. After that, Menotti's son Francis initially organized the festival, then a director appointed by the Italian Ministry of Culture took over.

Even though the golden days of the festival may be over now, it is worth visiting Spoleto during the festival, when the small town with its close to 38,000 inhabitants is transformed into a lively cultural center. Thanks to the amount of money that have been invested in the town in recent decades, and because many Romans have second homes here, Spoleto is now considered rather desirable and chic.

A CONCERT AT THE TEATRO ROMANO DURING THE ANNUAL FESTIVAL DEI DUE MONDI.

A CATHEDRAL SQUARE LIKE A STAGE SET

The historical city center recalls Roman times: ancient masonry peeks through here and there, and above all is the Arco di Druso, a large arch from the first century, stretching across a street in the old town. The Piazza del Duomo marks the town center, one of the most beautiful squares in Central Italy. You should absolutely approach it coming from the Via del Duomo. At a certain point of the street, an alleyway like a staircase, which gets wider with each step, leads down to the square. It's a descent with a "wow" factor!

The cathedral occupies the entire lower part of the square and is one of the most elegant Romanesque buildings in Italy. Built in the twelfth century, it boasts a façade with a richly decorated rose window and a pointed roof. The interior was renovated in the fifteenth century and houses important works of art, such as a portrait of Pope Urban VIII by baroque star Gian Lorenzo Bernini. The first chapel to the right is adorned with magnificent frescoes by the Renaissance painter Pinturicchio. Works by important artists can also be found in the other chapels, such as pieces by Filippo Lippi and Annibale Carracci. Lippi also created the grandiose murals of the apse. The altar is the work of Giuseppe Valadier, a master of the neoclassical period who was highly regarded throughout Europe.

The cathedral square is particularly buzzing during the festival. The symphonic concert on the final festival night takes place here, in the open air. At Tric Trac, the only café on the square, you get the chance to observe the hubbub close-up. Next to it, the Casa Menotti museum recounts the composer's life and work. The house used to be his home.

WHAT GOETHE RHAPSODIZED ABOUT

Above the cathedral square is the Basilica of Sant'Eufemia in the courtyard of the Episcopal Palace—a Romanesque gem. Built around the same time, San Gregorio Maggiore dazzles with beautiful frescoes from the thirteenth century, and San Nicolò with its cloisters in the early Gothic style. Spoleto also has several museums. The baroque Palazzo Collicola, for example, exhibits modern and contemporary art by Sol LeWitt, Alexander Calder, Henry Moore, and many others, who performed at the Festival dei Due Mondi.

Above the old town, in a prominent position, stands the mighty Rocca Albornoziana, a medieval castle that is now a museum. Concerts often take place in the castle courtyard. Behind it, one of the most impressive bridges in Europe spans across a valley with a stream. At 755 feet (230 meters) long, with a maximum height of 250 feet (76 meters), it is a masterpiece of medieval architecture, built between the thirteenth and the fourteenth centuries. Goethe, who put to paper his visit to Spoleto in his *Italian Journey*, was also fascinated by this construction.

Across the bridge is San Pietro, a Romanesque church of great beauty, built on the remains of a Roman temple. The façade, with its relief decorations, is particularly fascinating. A little outside the old town, behind the Piazza Vittorio, is San Salvatore. The early Christian basilica is one of the most impressive places of worship in the city.

ROMAN TEMPLE ON THE WATER

Between Spoleto and Foligno, approximately fifteen minutes by car, is a magical UNESCO World Heritage Site. In Roman times, a religious festival was celebrated at the Fonti del Clitunno in honor of Jupiter. A temple here is dedicated to him. This completely reconstructed ancient building is directly at the source of the Clitunno River. The mythical place was praised by Virgil and later by Lord Byron and the Italian national poet Giosuè Carducci. The temple is surrounded by nature and exudes a very bucolic atmosphere. Right by the river, the restaurant Fonti del Clitunno is worth a pit stop. Regional delicacies are available here, as are excellent Umbrian wines.

LEARN MORE
Spoleto: www.visitspoleto.it
Festival dei Due Mondi: www.festivaldispoleto.com
Fonti del Clitunno: www.fontidelclitunno.it

PITIGLIANO – ITALY'S JERUSALEM

AN EXAMPLE OF TOLERANCE

First the Etruscans, then the Romans, and later Christians and Jews, in a rare example of harmony: picturesque Pitigliano, hidden in the woods, proved that peaceful coexistence between religions is possible. Until the Nazis came . . .

Pitigliano became a refuge for Jewish people in the sixteenth century. Many believers fled Rome when a ghetto was established there. Between 1569 and 1593, around five hundred of them settled in this small village in the south of Tuscany—accounting for five hundred of the 6,000 inhabitants at that time. Pitigliano did not belong to the Papal States but rather to the religiously tolerant Tuscany of the Medicis. Here, Jews were allowed to live their faith and became an integrated part of the community. Many Jewish citizens led the way in agriculture, business, and cultural life. When Italy was unified in the nineteenth century, many Jewish residents left Pitigliano to seek their luck in the big cities. But it was ultimately the German occupiers who ensured—one hundred years later—that even the last Jews disappeared from Pitigliano.

IN SEARCH OF JEWISH TRACES

It was not until the end of the 1990s that Jewish life began to flourish again in Pitigliano. If you wander through the picturesque historical center of the small town of almost 4,000 inhabitants nowadays, you will come across various buildings owned by the Jewish community that have been painstakingly restored and can be visited. This has created an impressive monument to the centuries-long coexistence. The sixteenth-century synagogue, the community oven, and various stores in the Jewish quarter, as well as an interesting museum dedicated to many facets of the local Jewish history, are

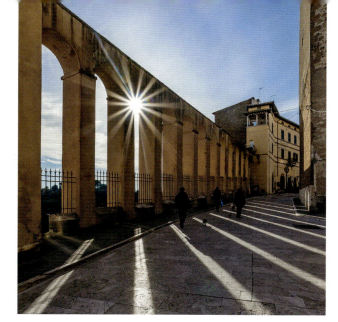

OPPOSITE: THE ETRUSCANS FOUNDED PITIGLIANO ON A LARGE TUFF ROCK PLATEAU. *FAR LEFT*: THE ENTRANCE TO THE HISTORICAL OLD TOWN IS THE FIRST SIGN THAT YOU CAN'T GET FAR HERE BY CAR. *LEFT*: THE SOFT TUFF ROCK HAS BEEN USED FOR CRAFTSMANSHIP SINCE ETRUSCAN TIMES.

worth a sightseeing tour. These buildings are located in the medieval town center, which has barely changed over the centuries. A stroll here is particularly appealing, because it is very quiet and you still feel a little like an explorer, since this part of Tuscany has never been overrun by tourists.

ETRUSCAN HERITAGE

Besides the Jewish monuments, there are many other sights as well. The Palazzo Orsini is an impressive fortress, which dates back to the eleventh century and was renovated and extended by the princes of Tuscany at the end of the nineteenth century. The fortress now houses the Diocesan Museum. It provides testament that people in the countryside also invested a lot of money in embellishing religious garments and sacred art.

Of course, there is also a theater. The Teatro Salvini dates from 1823 and was restored in the 1970s. Among the numerous churches in Pitigliano, the Cattedrale di Santi Pietro e Paolo stands out; it received its current appearance in the seventeenth century. The interior is coherently designed in a baroque style.

There is a town wall, too, of course. The "new" wall from the tenth century was erected on the remains of the Etruscan wall, which dates back to the seventh century BCE. Those who climb up to Pitigliano on foot—the town is located at an altitude of about 1,115 feet (340 meters) on a rugged tuff hill surrounded by vineyards and dense forests with holm oaks—will get to see several caves in the tuff rock. These probably used to be Etruscan tombs, and they have since served local winemakers as excellently air-conditioned wine cellars.

A PATH THROUGH THE ROCK

In the immediate vicinity of Pitigliano, visitors get the chance to walk to picturesque Etruscan necropolises, hidden among the lush greenery, such as the Necropoli di Gradione and the Necropoli di San Giovanni and San Giuseppe. But there is another unique site from ancient times: between the towns of Pitigliano, Sovana, and Sorano, there are roads through nature that the Etruscans carved from the rocks. Instead of walking around the soft tuff rocks, the Etruscans simply cut through them. The walls to the left and right are straight and feel smooth to the touch. A total of four Etruscan rock roads, called Via Cave, can be discovered here.

LEARN MORE
Pitigliano: www.pitigliano.org
Museo ebraico: www.museidimaremma.it

THE BRIGHT FAÇADE OF THE HIGH GOTHIC CATHEDRAL OF ORVIETO (*THIS PAGE*) IS UNIQUE IN ITALY—JUST LIKE THE POZZO DI SAN PANCRAZIO WITH ITS DOUBLE SPIRAL STAIRCASE THAT DESCENDS DEEP INTO THE EARTH (*OPPOSITE*).

ORVIETO – A FIRST-CLASS DESTINATION
FASCINATING FAÇADE

As a rule, Italy travelers pass this small town by on their way to Rome—even though it is one of the most beautiful cities in southern Umbria, historically intact and rich in architectural monuments, notably its cathedral.

The city skyline deserves to be approached from the country roads of the surrounding area. This is the only way to fully experience the spectacular view. The entire old town is located on a soft tuff rock plateau, crisscrossed by tunnels and hollowed out with cellars, cisterns, and tombs since the Etruscan era.

Thus, a fascinating underground labyrinth was formed that can be visited today. About 3,000 years of digging into the tuff rock underneath the city have created stairwells and small squares that are magnificently showcased in the dark. Since the late nineteenth century, this 0.6-mile-long (1 kilometer) labyrinth has been excavated, explored, and rendered accessible. Visitors are generally allowed to enter the underground city as part of a guided group. Since Etruscan times, people have inhabited the hill above. The Romans came here, as did the Pope in 1527; at that time, Pope Clement VII fled to Orvieto from Emperor Charles V's soldiers as they were looting Rome.

Orvieto's historical center is abundant in significant monuments. The cathedral is undoubtedly one of the most beautiful and idiosyncratic in Italy. Its Gothic façade, with its peaks and beautiful decorations, dominates the entire old town.

Construction began in 1288. The famous architect and artist Arnolfo di Cambio is said to have come up with the design; he was the same master architect who later built the Florentine cathedral and the Palazzo Vecchio. The enormous building was not finished until the fourteenth century.

A VERTICAL THEATER SET

The façade of the cathedral alone is worth the drive. There is nothing quite like it in all of Italy. It combines the northern European Gothic style of French cathedrals with a characteristically Italian emphasis on surfaces in a fascinating way. Its design is marked by multicolored mosaics and bas-reliefs. This makes the façade resemble a huge, impenetrable theater set that is best viewed with binoculars to experience it in all its detail.

The decorations on the façade are complemented by large wall reliefs on the piers of the cathedral. They are the work of an anonymous artist of the early fourteenth century and cover a total area of more than 1,184 square feet (110 square meters). It depicts the biblical story of the origin of humankind. Although this is clearly medieval art, these sophisticated representations show to what extent Italian sculptors of the time were influenced by antiquity.

The design of the cathedral's interior also includes highlights of art history. First of all, there is the color scheme: the columns and walls are in keeping with a black-and-white theme, featuring horizontal stripes. The apse boasts beautiful frescoes from the fourteenth and fifteenth centuries.

FRESCOES THAT INSPIRED MICHELANGELO

However, visitors will find the most beautiful frescoes in the San Brizio Chapel. It is here that Renaissance artist Luca Signorelli created a key piece of Italian art history. Countless figures—earthly and heavenly—are employed to depict the story of the Antichrist, complete with the end of the world, death, hell, and paradise. All this is rendered in an extremely realistic style and has been perfectly preserved.

LEFT: **SMALL BRIDGES LEAD ACROSS THE ROMANTIC ALLEYWAYS, CONNECTING HOUSES WITH THEIR GARDENS.** *ABOVE*: **PAYING ATTENTION TO DETAIL—SUCH AS MEDIEVAL DECORATIVE ART, IN THIS CASE—IS WELL WORTH IT IN MANY OF ORVIETO'S CHURCHES.**

LEFT: **THE OLD TOWN IS BATHED IN GOLDEN SUNLIGHT DURING LATE SUMMER DAYS.**

A stroll through Orvieto's medieval maze of alleyways and squares, which have been surprisingly well preserved, is very appealing. Most secular buildings, especially the palaces of local noble families, are severe looking and may even exude a hostile effect on visitors. One example is the Palazzo Soliano. Built in the thirteenth century, it is more reminiscent of a fortress than a palace. The building houses the Museo dell'Opera del Duomo. This museum is fairly important, given that it exhibits precious works by Luca Signorelli, Simone Martini, Andrea Pisano, and other masters of the thirteenth and fourteenth centuries.

The Palazzo del Popolo is a fine example of a civic palace built in the mid-thirteenth century. Even though the huge building was altered with historical embellishments during a nineteenth-century restoration, it still gives off a powerful impression.

WONDERFUL WELL

Another Orvieto oddity is the Pozzo di San Patrizio. This well was carved out of the soft tuff rock beneath the city by Renaissance master builder Antonio da Sangallo the Younger in the first half of the sixteenth century. The circular well is about 197 feet (60 meters) deep and has a diameter of 43 feet (13 meters). What makes it so special is that Sangallo designed it as two spiral staircases in the shape of a double helix, leading from top to bottom and back up. The stairs never meet, so in earlier times, pack animals such as donkeys could climb down with empty containers and others could return with filled loads without encountering each other or getting in each other's way.

The walls of each of the spiral staircases are interrupted by seventy-two windows. This ensures that natural light from above penetrates far into the depth. Take the time to descend all the way to the bottom. This well gives an absolutely fascinating impression.

MIDDLE AGES WITH MODERN COMFORTS

The drive takes about forty minutes and guides you through a truly bucolic landscape. Your destination is the Castello di Proceno, a medieval castle and a tiny village with only a few alleyways and houses, built on a rock. The castle's owner, Cecilia Cecchini Bisoni, known as Donna Pucci, offers cozy furnished and comfortable guest rooms in the historic buildings. Every room is different. Donna is also a gifted cook. Her specialty: reviving recipes from the Renaissance. In the winter, patrons dine in an Etruscan cave turned restaurant; in the summertime, in a garden pavilion by the pool.

LEARN MORE
Orvieto: www.orvietoviva.com
Castello di Proceno: www.castellodiproceno.it

CIVITA DI BAGNOREGIO – A VILLAGE IN A TOP LOCATION

CRUMBLING BEAUTY

This mighty and nearly 985-foot-tall (300 meters) tuff rock cone, surrounded by a green hilly landscape, is crowned by a picture-perfect village. This miniature town features historical buildings, a central piazza, and a fantastic view.

A truly remote place. As a suburb of the municipality of Bagnoregio, it is located near the border between Lazio and Umbria, east of the deep Lake Bolsena. Civita di Bagnoregio is not accessible by car or even by moped; the only access is via an 820-foot-long (250 meters) pedestrian bridge from the town of Bagnoregio. In the seventh century BCE, the Etruscans settled on this hill, which continues to be a picturesque and—since it is traffic-free—tranquil village.

A MEETING POINT FOR PRIESTS AND KINGS

The place hides many secrets; respectable researchers of the Etruscan period do not rule out that the ancient Fanum Voltumnae may have been located at exactly the spot where Civita now is. This mysterious place was where the political and religious leaders of the twelve Etruscan cities met each year in a temple to discuss the future fate of their people. What is certain is that the Roman consul Marcus Fulvius Flaccus had the Etruscan settlement destroyed in 264 BCE. The history of Civita only picked up again in the Middle Ages. From then on, the village belonged to the Papal States and became the residence of a bishop.

A walk through Civita is simply magical. At the end of the footbridge, visitors pass through the Porta Santa Maria. This gate is part of the ancient medieval fortification of Civita.

SEEN QUICKLY, REMAINING FOR AGES

The hamlet is home to no more than twenty people nowadays and offers narrow paved alleyways and the

church of San Donato on the eponymous square. The ancient forum is said to have been located beneath this house of worship, a cathedral and bishop's church active from the sixth century to the end of the seventeenth century. It guards a beautiful and well-preserved crucifix by Donatello's workshop in the fifteenth century.

Several city palaces, including the bishop's, frame the small square. The Palazzo Mazzocchi-Alemanni, built in the Renaissance, exhibits Etruscan and Roman finds excavated from the soft tuff hill and the immediate surroundings.

There is a restaurant, a coffee bar, and a few options of accommodations to spend the night in Civita. Staying over has a very special appeal. When the few day tourists have left, the village falls into a deep slumber: no noise, no car horns—only birdsong and the presence of a few people. Sunset from one of the panoramic views of Civita is unforgettable. Add a glass of wine, and it is perfect bliss.

DYING CITY

But Civita is dying—a little more with every bad weather front. The hamlet is crumbling, and heavy rain is its worst enemy. The porous tuff stone crumbles easily, and it tumbles into the deep valley underneath Civita, piece by piece. Some of the old buildings are already under threat of collapse. Even though erosion makes the tuff hill look extremely attractive, it still represents a great danger for Civita.

Although in recent years, mostly US visitors have come here (a US university organizes summer courses in Civita), the hamlet is usually empty and visited by few tourists. It's the ideal place to get some rest and relax for a while.

OPPOSITE: **A DREAM OF A VILLAGE, LOCATED ON A STEEP ROCK PLATEAU AND SURROUNDED BY KARST FORMATIONS.** *BELOW*: **THE SMALL VILLAGE SQUARE IS THE CENTER OF CIVITA DI BAGNOREGIO, LOCATED ON A FRAGILE ROCK.**

MONTEFIASCONE – WINE AND OTHER QUALITIES

Less than a twenty-minute drive from Civita di Bagnoregio, the small town of Montefiascone towers on a hill above the picturesque Lake Bolsena. It is the place of origin of a light white wine called Est! Est!! Est!!! The name dates back to 1111. Tourists should certainly pay San Flaviano a visit, as it is one of the most beautiful and unusual—from an architectural perspective—Romanesque churches in the Lazio region. The façade features three large arches, and the interior impresses with imaginatively painted capitals depicting saints and monsters on the columns. The enormous interior opens up to the upper church. Built in the thirteenth century, this holy place has barely changed. The Rocca city fortress provides stunning views over the large lake.

LEARN MORE
Civita di Bagnoregio: www.civitadibagnoregio.it
Montefiascone: www.tusciaturismo.com

BOMARZO – A FANTASTICAL SPOT IN THE COUNTRY

MYSTERIOUS GHOULS

Long before amusement parks attracted the masses in the twentieth century, a nobleman created his very own magical park in Central Italy. The Parco dei Mostri is a very special place that even now, five hundred years later, still surprises and entices.

Its huge mouth is wide open. And the monstrous face's eyes are staring down. In the dark recess of the open mouth, there are two single teeth. Over the years, a branch has grown across the grotesque face. Stairs with weathered steps lead up to the maw. The dense greenery of trees and plants surrounds the monster's round face. Another mythical creature also has its mouth agape. Is it human or animal? Who knows? It is balancing a large ball on its head. It's a fantastical creature, perhaps the product of its inventor's nightmares.

It is impossible to stand upright in the little two-story house. Erected leaning to one side, it threatens to fall over any moment. A gigantic turtle appears behind the trees. Dragons hide in the park's thicket, a colossal sculpture of a naked woman called Echidna has two snakes in the place where her outstretched legs should be, and an elephant is carrying a castle tower while seemingly devouring a soldier. Using its trunk, the animal pushes the man deep down its throat.

A CHALLENGING PARK

At every turn, visitors to the Gardens of Bomarzo—also known as Sacro Bosco, the "sacred grove"—discover these sculptures, some of which are a few feet tall. In 1547, the architect and second-hand book dealer Pirro Ligorio designed this wonderful

OPPOSITE: **RENAISSANCE DISNEYLAND: THE CREEPY GARDEN OF BOMARZO IS UNIQUE WORLDWIDE.** *LEFT:* **THE PARK'S LANDSCAPE ALSO INCLUDES THIS LITTLE TEMPLE; NO ONE QUITE KNOWS WHAT IT WAS USED FOR.**

garden on behalf of the extravagant art connoisseur Duke Pier Francesco Orsini.

In doing so, he mixed ideas of characters from ancient mythology with plenty of grotesque fantasy. With characteristic aristocratic understatement, the duke simply called the strange park "giardino," the garden, and dedicated it to his late wife, Giulia Farnese, who died very young. This surreal estate filled with monsters and bizarre—sometimes even obscene—sculptures would inspire later generations of artists, such as the Spanish surrealist Salvador Dalí. The aim of these creations is to confuse visitors and put their ideas of morality, imagination, perspective, and aesthetics to the test.

Many of the sculptures were inspired by literary characters in works by Francesco Petrarca, Bernardo Tasso, and, above all, in the romance of chivalry *Orlando Furioso* by Ludovico Ariosto. This was literature that every well-educated person of the time would have read.

FOREVER MYSTERIOUS

The park is about 7.4 acres (3 hectares) in size. It is located in the middle of the forest, north of the small town of Bomarzo. To this day, people puzzle over why the prince created such a grotesque garden. Some experts are convinced that he used it to introduce intimate friends to the rites of an even more secretive private club. Or maybe he just wanted to impress his guests. After all, grotesquerie, the bizarre, and curiosities characterized the dominant style of his time: Mannerism.

The park also includes a mysterious temple, il Tempio. It combines architectural elements from various periods. What did the duke do here? Did he host parties? Organize orgies? Organize secret initiation rites, or simply lavish banquets? No one knows. The duke did not leave anything behind in writing about his fantasy garden—perhaps intentionally. So it is entirely up to visitors to make of it what they want.

VILLA LANTE – GEOMETRIC GARDEN GAMES

The famous Renaissance architect Jacopo Barozzi da Vignola is said to have designed this garden near the village of Bagnaia in 1566. It is part of the wealthy Alessandro Cardinal Peretti's country house. The park consists of terraces that nestle onto a hillside. Ramps and stairs lead up and down the slope. A sophisticated system of wells and streams supplies the water features. The park has a single theme: the rediscovery of paradise lost. This Garden of Eden was invented by the architect da Vignola. It displays the typical notion of the time: nature as completely subordinate to humankind.

LEARN MORE
Park of the Monsters / Parco dei Mostri: www.sacrobosco.it
Villa Lante: www.polomusealelazio.beniculturali.it

TUSCANIA – LAZIO'S BRIGHT NORTH
ETRUSCAN DISCOVERIES

A gem of a small town! After a walk around Tuscania, you'd be tempted to buy a holiday home here, preferably one with a view of the hilly surroundings with their Etruscan ruins and Romanesque churches. It's a place where historical heritage is still intact.

Cars must be parked outside, beyond the completely preserved city walls; only pedestrians are allowed to enter, through one of the historical city gates. And they'll immediately dive into a setting that could not be more enticing. Those living here, it seems, inhabit a kind of stage made for cheerful Rossini operas.

IN THE OLD TOWN MAZE

The historical town center is located within the medieval walls. These are over 3 miles (5 kilometers) long and equipped with several hefty towers. Narrow streets and alleys alternate with squares and tight corners. A surprise is waiting around every corner: a church or chapel here, a plain palazzo, a hardware or mom-and-pop store there, or an inviting café or restaurant. It is no surprise that a lot of Romans own holiday homes here.

In the San Giacomo cathedral, make sure to visit the chapel at the end of the nave. The late Gothic painter Andrea di Bartolo, a true expert, created the winged altar and other altar paintings.

PARK WITH A VIEW

Less than a five-minute walk away, behind the cathedral, towers the Torre di Lavello, with a well-kept park stretching out behind it. The view of the landscape makes for a surprise effect: on top of the surrounding hills are the churches San Pietro and Santa Maria Maggiore. Art lovers travel to Tuscania for these two Romanesque churches alone. San Pietro is flanked by two medieval towers and presents itself nowadays as a large church from the eleventh to the thirteenth centuries. On the square in front of the church, surrounded by many other old buildings, you feel like you are in a historical movie!

OPPOSITE: AN ETRUSCAN FUNERARY SCULPTURE IS LYING IN THE FOREGROUND. *LEFT*: NOT UNCOMMON IN TUSCANIA: EARLY CHRISTIAN VAULTS WITH ANTIQUE COLUMNS ERECTED ABOVE FORMER ETRUSCAN BUILDINGS. *BELOW*: THE ROMANESQUE CHIESA SAN PIETRO IS ALSO BUILT ON TOP OF AN ETRUSCAN TEMPLE.

ARTFUL COLUMN RECYCLING

Above the plain Gothic main portal is an elegant rose window, surrounded by the symbols of the four Evangelists. The building was erected above an Etruscan necropolis. The interior, with its nave and two aisles, looks extremely harmonious. The floor is a work by the Cosmatis. This family of craftspeople worked in Rome and the surrounding area in the thirteenth century. They sawed antique columns of different sizes and colors into flat disks and used these to create this floor, an immensely beautiful work of art. The church's crypt is a simple room with columns and the remains of Roman masonry. The view of Tuscania from the square in front of the church is magnificent; not a single modern building disrupts the sight!

The construction of Santa Maria Maggiore began in the eighth century. The present design dates back to the thirteenth and fourteenth centuries. The main portal—one of three—is richly decorated. The decorative figures were created in different periods. They include the four Evangelists, lions, a Madonna with child, the Binding of Isaac, and the Lamb of God. The nave and the two aisles in the church interior are supported by Romanesque columns. While the frescoes are not very well preserved, there is a remarkable depiction of a devil. He can be easily spotted in the arch at the apse, eating the sinners and leaving behind whatever is left of them at the end of his digestive tract.

A little outside Tuscania, the well-preserved tombs of wealthy Etruscans, occasionally painted with frescoes, are worth a visit. In the Necropoli di Madonna dell'Olivo, the Tomba della Regina—the queen's grave—stands out in particular. This tomb received its name due to its size and its columns, which are carved straight out of the surrounding rock. The necropolis includes various tombs from the Etruscan era as well as from the later Hellenistic period.

MORE THAN TEN CHAIRS

Take a small square, not far from the municipal park, and add some old houses, a good dose of tranquility, an overgrown leafy pergola, a few tables with brightly painted chairs, and a host who knows what he is doing. The Ristorante Dieci Sedie, the "ten chairs" restaurant, on the Piazza Largo Della Neve 2, is an inside tip in Tuscania. For a fixed price of around 40 euros per person, guests are served a plentiful menu of fish and meat, side dishes, and desserts, plus delicious wine and mineral water. You are advised to arrive hungry enough after an extensive sightseeing tour to eat it all. The nicest seats are outside, on a mellow evening. Every single dish is delicious, making this the perfect place to end a day in Tuscania.

LEARN MORE
Tuscania: www.tusciaturismo.com

TARQUINIA – A CEMETERY WITH AN ADJACENT SMALL TOWN

DESCENT INTO THE REALM OF THE DEAD

Visitors come to Tarquinia in northwestern Lazio mainly because of its Etruscan necropolis, a designated UNESCO World Heritage Site since 2004. But before or after your visit with the dead, make sure to stroll through the charming historical center of this Etruscan settlement.

Tarquinia was founded as one of about a dozen Etruscan city-states in Central Italy. It was protected by a 5-mile-long (8 kilometers) city wall as early as the fifth century BCE. Nowadays, the old town has a medieval look, through and through. Characteristic of the Lazio region north of Rome, almost all of the town's buildings were made from the local dark tuff stone, an easily malleable type of volcanic rock with tiny to small holes.

ART FOR THE LIVING . . .

Palazzo Vitelleschi from the Renaissance, or, more precisely, the Museo Archeologico Nazionale di Tarquinia that it houses, exhibits Etruscan art treasures that have been excavated in the village and its surrounding area. Among them is the Bocchoris vase, an elegant Etruscan ceramic vase of 8.7 inches (22 centimeters) from the eighth century BCE, which is decorated with Egyptian-style motifs. The town, with its population of just over 16,000, also invites a visit to the Church of Santa Maria di Castello. Built in the twelfth century, the ground inside this church is covered with an elegant and stunning Cosmatesque mosaic floor from the early Gothic period.

. . . AND FOR THE DEAD

Outside Tarquinia lies the UNESCO World Heritage Site of the Etruscan Necropolis of Monterozzi. It is internationally renowned for its 6,100 tombs carved into the rocks, of which about 150 are painted. Sloped ramps lead down to the large underground tomb chambers. All of these tombs are idyllically

located in nature, making a visit to this cemetery very charming indeed.

A number of these vaults were relatively spacious, probably designed for couples. Almost all of them date from the eighth to the fourth centuries BCE, the heyday of Etruscan culture—before it was "swallowed up" by the Romans.

INSIGHT INTO THE LIFE OF THE NOBILITY

Three Etruscan tombs are notably beautiful because they are particularly well preserved. The Tomba delle Leonesse, the tomb of the lionesses, from the fourth century is a small chamber with a roof. The mural depicts flying birds and a sketched sea with floating and jumping dolphins. The hunter's grave, the Tomba del Cacciatore, appears like the inside of a tent. And the Tomba della Caccia e della Pesca, the tomb dedicated to hunting and fishing, consists of two halls with frescoes, representing a rather Dionysian dance of free abandon in a forest that was deemed sacred, according to archaeologists. Visitors can also marvel at very well-preserved hunting and fishing scenes. In addition, the owners of the tomb were immortalized here in portraits.

Although the Etruscan tombs are very close together, elegant cypresses and bushes have managed to grow in the gaps between them. Make sure to wear sturdy footwear, even on warm days; although the necropolis seems like a peaceful countryside space, you could easily encounter snakes and scorpions here.

Many graves show depictions of the lives of wealthy Etruscans. The pictures reflect the lifestyles of the rich and famous able to afford these tombs: hunts and dances, lavish banquets, and athletic competitions held in honor of the dead at their funeral celebrations. Thus, these paintings introduce visitors to the ways of life of a people who have left very few written documents behind.

OPPOSITE: **ETRUSCAN TEMPLES AND TOMBS ARE A TESTIMONY TO THE ERSTWHILE IMPORTANCE OF TARQUINIA.** LEFT: **THE OLD TOMB CHAMBERS ARE OFTEN DECORATED WITH LARGE-SCALE MURALS.** ABOVE: **THE MUNICIPAL MUSEUM EXHIBITS ANTIQUE TREASURES PRISED FROM THE EARTH.**

TRIP TO THE LIDO

It takes only a quarter of an hour by car to travel from this small town to the beach. Lido di Tarquinia is the name of the flat stretch by the sea with its wide, long, and very clean sandy beaches. The best time to swim here is in the late afternoon, when most visitors are gone and you have the beach almost to yourself. After that, we recommend a meal in a local restaurant such as the Ristorante Lupo di Mare. It is part of a stylish lido and sets up tables right next to its pool, which is lit up in the evening—very romantic indeed. The wine menu features excellent white wines from the local mountains.

LEARN MORE
Tarquinia: www.tarquiniaturismo.it
Necropoli di Tarquinia: www.necropoliditarquinia.it
Lupo di Mare: www.grandhotelhelios.it

CAPRAROLA – A MANNERIST MANIFESTO

THE FARNESES' PARADISE

North of Rome, a majestic palace one would usually expect in a large city rises in and above the village of Caprarola. It's a country residence full of magnificent paintings, gorgeous halls, and an artificial park grotto.

Why go to Caprarola? It is a pretty village like countless others in the northern Lazio region, about an hour's drive from Rome. But the upper part of the hill on which the village is built is topped with a magnificent palace—a celebration of Mannerism!

UNBRIDLED WILL OF CONSTRUCTION

The Palazzo Farnese, named after the commissioning family, is considered one of the most important palaces of the Italian late Renaissance. And that is saying something in a country rich in remarkable palaces! Almost all the rooms the Farneses used as state rooms are painted with frescoes in the Mannerist style, the art genre that followed the Renaissance before the baroque style became fashionable.

There once was a fortress on a pentagonal base on the location of the current palazzo—on the southeastern slope of Monti Cimini in the Cimini mountains, which are still densely covered with woods. Cardinal Alessandro Farnese, very appreciative of art, began construction on these foundations around 1520. He commissioned star architect Antonio da Sangallo with the project. But then the cardinal was elected pope and renamed himself Paul III; the construction work came to a halt. It was ten years after the pope's death that work continued. The new head of the House of Farnese, who

OPPOSITE: THE PALAZZO FARNESE TOWERS OVER THE VILLAGE OF CAPRAROLA LIKE A FORTRESS. *LEFT*: THE CEILING DEPICTING THE CONSTELLATIONS IN THE SALA DEL MAPPAMONDO IS ONE OF THE MANSION'S MOST BEAUTIFUL FRESCOES.

was also called Alessandro Farnese and who was also a cardinal, turned the planned fortress into a gorgeous and very impressive country residence. He was fond of this place, which his doctors recommended to him on account of the fresh country air.

OF FRESCOES AND SOPHISTICATION

The palace, in its current iteration, is a pentagon, and it is a masterpiece by the Bologna architect Giacomo Barozzi da Vignola. The five-sided palace has a simple yet elegant—and also pentagonal—courtyard with colonnades. The individual stories are connected by spiral stairs. The landlord's private chambers are reached via the most beautiful of staircases, the so-called Scala Regia.

All the main halls, the stairwells, the corridors, and the large loggia overlooking the town of Caprarola are decorated with murals. They are considered to be the best-preserved examples of Italian Mannerism. Some of the most distinguished artists of their time contributed frescoes, including the brothers Federico and Taddeo Zuccari, a young El Greco, and Jacopo Bertoia. Besides the many historical scenes that glorify the actions of the Farnese family, as well as biblical, mythological, and allegorical depictions, it is the many curious representations that stand out. They are so-called grotesque paintings, a type of ornamentation based on fantastical plants, animals, and humanoid figures. This type of art was very popular in the sixteenth century. It is said that Raphael reinvented it following ancient models.

The Scala Regia and the "piano nobile," that is, the palazzo's principal floor, are so abundantly painted, from floor to ceiling, that they simply render visitors speechless. The most impressive room is doubtlessly the Sala del Mappamondo, which features huge maps painted on the walls and an enormous ceiling with a celestial map and zodiac signs.

SURPRISES HIDDEN IN THE GARDEN

A small drawbridge leads visitors from the magnificent halls to the park of the Palazzo Farnese. This classic Italian garden hides several surprises. First of all, there is the perfectly mown geometrical lawn. Through a small woodland, you reach the Catena d'acqua, a narrow water cascade. At its end, on a hill, is the "casino." The elegant summer house, with its three-arched loggia, was designed for relaxation; it's the work of Jacopo del Duca. It goes without saying that the inside of this garden cottage, which is almost the size of a small palace, is adorned with murals.

LEARN MORE
Caprarola: www.visitcaprarola.it
Palazzo Farnese: www.polomusealelazio.beniculturali.it

SAN CLEMENTE A CASAURIA – THE NATIONAL MONUMENT
THE POWER OF SIMPLICITY

Is a church sufficient as a destination? Yes, because this abbey is one of the most impressive churches in Central Italy. It's a sacred treasure of architecture that has been restored to its former splendor after the devastating earthquake of 2009.

The Abbazia in the Abruzzo has been awarded the title of Italian National Monument due to its architectural history and its beauty. It is also a papal church, since the Abbazia di San Clemente a Casauria has been the final resting place of the relics of Pope Clement I since the distant year 782 CE. The monastery was founded a mere year earlier, by Louis II, the king of the Langobards, who ruled over Italy back then. Soon after, a long chain of destructions took its course.

A HISTORY OF DESTRUCTION
In 910 CE, the North African Saracens destroyed the monastery in the Abruzzo. After this traumatic event, the monastery was fortified with walls. In 1076, the Normans invaded the complex and destroyed it again. In the twelfth century, the monastery gained its present appearance—as one of the most beautiful and famous architectural monuments in all of Central Italy.

The monastery was probably erected on the remains of a Roman temple. At least, that is what claimed by the two monks who wrote a chronicle of the monastery in the Middle Ages. Various earthquakes caused the monastery and the church to collapse. In 1348, the region was particularly badly hit. Eventually, only the church was rebuilt. It was restored in the early twentieth century.

ELEGANT INTERIOR

The building's exterior and interior demonstrate the architectural harmony of which Gothic craftspeople in Italy were capable. The bronze portal is a marvel in itself. There are two gates dating from the late twelfth century, both of which are almost intact. The portal is located underneath the three-arched façade.

The interior is kept plain and simple, almost severe, yet extremely elegant. The pulpit is considered a work of the late twelfth century. It is a lectern for preaching from the Scriptures, decorated with the symbols of the Evangelists Mark and John. The Easter candelabra dates from the thirteenth century and is a magnificent large candlestick that once held the Easter candle and twelve more candles.

The ciborium, a stone canopy under which the altar is located, consists of ancient columns and a richly decorated square structure covered by a five-part dome. It dates back to the thirteenth century. The altar itself is a former pagan sarcophagus. No wonder: with all the ancient remains found in the area, medieval builders recycled them as building materials. The groups of columns supporting the wooden ceiling structure can be dated to the prehistoric period. They already hint at the Gothic period, which would later reach its heights in French architecture.

OPPOSITE: **RESTORED TO ITS FORMER SPLENDOR: SAN CLEMENTE A CASAURIA AFTER ITS RECONSTRUCTION.** BELOW: **DESIGN ELEMENTS FROM THE ROMANESQUE AND EARLY GOTHIC PERIODS HARMONIZE IN THE CHURCH INTERIOR.**

A CRYPT WITH SAWED-OFF COLUMNS

Underground, beneath the abbey church, visitors can go into the crypt. Here, the apse of a former church from the ninth century is clearly visible. To support the vaulted ceiling, Roman columns from the surrounding area were employed. They were quickly sawed off, and only their upper parts, with the richly decorated capitals, were used. This crypt is a magical place with its thick arches and shortened columns—despite the complete lack of paintings and other decorations.

THE SAFFRON CAPITAL

Not far from the abbey church, about thirty minutes by car, is where the best saffron in the world is harvested—according to Italian chefs. In Navelli, almost all of its roughly 500 inhabitants make their living by cultivating this delicate, slightly bitter-tasting, spicy, and tangy plant of the *Crocus* genus. The filaments of the flowers, which are still harvested by hand, are the "red gold" of the Abruzzo. They are processed into a spice that is certainly not cheap, but Italy's chefs simply swear by it. You can try it for yourself in Navelli, in one of a handful of rustic and cozy restaurants that offer hearty dishes with saffron. One of them is the Ristorante Antica Taverna, where the saffron filaments also flavor desserts.

LEARN MORE
San Clemente a Casauria:
www.musei.abruzzo.beniculturali.it
Ristorante Antica Taverna: www.anticataverna.it

ROME UNDERGROUND
A VERY DIFFERENT ETERNAL CITY

Below street level of the Italian capital, a completely different city awaits: one without noise, traffic jams, or natural light. In some places, you may go underground to discover a seemingly forgotten world of antiquity and the Middle Ages.

Rome is outstandingly beautiful but also very noisy, and local politicians are trying in vain to get its chaotic traffic under control. There is also a steadily high level of air pollution, and its smog often lingers for months. Those who need respite from this kind of Rome and are looking for the Eternal City—its enigmatic, sleepy, and truly unusual spots—must descend deep into the earth.

DESCENT IN THE PASTA FACTORY

There is a Rome beneath the Rome aboveground. Parts of it can be visited. And visitors to Rome can be sure that this Rome is certainly not crowded. Most tourists do not even know it exists. Right next to the Circus Maximus, the remains of the largest ancient chariot-racing stadium, is the former pasta factory Pastificio Pantanella. Underneath it, visitors enter the basement and the Mitreo del Circo Massimo. Parallel to early Christian worship, Mithra, a deity associated with the Middle East, was honored here. This underground site was discovered and excavated in the 1930s. Another room with sarcophagi and decorations illustrates the cult of the Mithraic mysteries.

The Mithraeum under Santa Prisca on the Aventine Hill is also magnificent. This place of worship dates back to the third century CE. Next to the banquet hall, where the disciples of this cult had their ritual meal, is a series of halls decorated with polychrome sculptures. A curious specimen is a statue depicting the god Mithra killing a bull, which is a typical representation in this cult.

Another impressive place of the Mithra cult is located right beneath the baroque church of San

OPPOSITE: **THE ROMAN FORUM IS THE HEART OF THE ANCIENT MEGA-METROPOLIS.** *THIS PAGE*: **THIS SUBTERRANEAN MITHRAEUM ONCE SERVED AS A PLACE OF WORSHIP TO THE GOD MITHRA.**

Clemente. From the interior of the church, visitors first descend into an early Christian sanctuary; then, further down is another set of stairs to the grotto.

BIRD DEPICTIONS FOR THE DEAD
Close to the Galleria Borghese, with its art treasures, visitors are invited to go underground to explore the Ipogeo di Via Livenza. This space is a hypogeum, an underground vault that served as a burial chamber. In this case, the underground structure measures 69 by 23 feet (21 by 7 meters) and extends across various rooms. Walls and recesses are decorated with well-preserved mosaics and paintings. Among them are early Christian allegorical depictions of birds and Erotes. Peter the Apostle is also portrayed, drawing water from a rock to baptize a pagan Roman soldier. In addition to early Christian representations, pagan figures such as the hunting goddess Diana also stand out.

Beneath the Palazzo Valentino, in which the German baroque composer George Frideric Handel once lived and worked as a guest hosted by the prince Ruspoli, and where the administration of the Lazio region is now housed, there is an entire ancient Roman residence. The Domus Romane di Palazzo Valentini lies 23 feet (7 meters) below today's street level. These are the well-preserved remains of a stately urban villa from the first to the fourth centuries CE, inclusive of private thermal baths and murals. You can also explore the remains of a temple, probably dedicated to the deified Emperor Trajan.

THE QUEEN OF THE CATACOMBS
The numerous intact catacombs of Rome are very well known. They are open to visitors, and many include them in their trip to Rome. Among the lesser visited, yet most fascinating, is the Catacomb

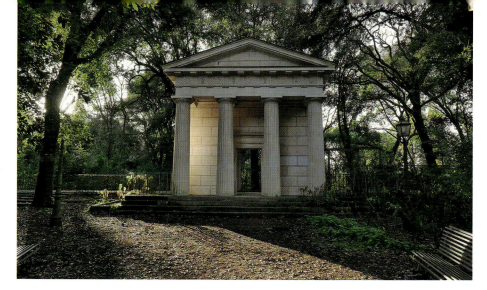

OPPOSITE: **THE ROMAN ELITE ONCE RESIDED IN THIS MANSION UNDERNEATH THE PALAZZO VALENTINI.**
LEFT: **THE NEOCLASSICAL FLORA TEMPLE STANDS DREAMILY IN THE ROMAN CITY PARK VILLA ADA.**
BELOW: **THE ENTRANCE TO THE CATACOMBS OF SAN CALLISTO HAS AN ALMOST RURAL FEEL.**

of Priscilla. It is located on the Via Salaria, next to the second largest city park in Rome, which is part of the Villa Ada district.

The underground corridors of this catacomb are 8 miles (13 kilometers) long and branch out into countless underground galleries. It is not without reason that this burial site is called the "Queen of the Roman Catacombs." This is also because nowhere else in Rome did so many martyrs of the early Christian church find their final resting place. High vaults and halls open up here, and there are staircases and countless murals, including one of the first representations of Christ in art history. Animals, figures, saints, and one tomb after another . . .

For some time now, the site underneath the famous Baths of Caracalla, the ruins of the largest public bath of ancient times, can also be visited. There are enormous rooms where the fire was lit for the warm-water baths above. The Colosseum also features underground spaces where the wild animals were kept for the hunt that took place aboveground and where gladiators got ready for their death matches. Visitors can marvel at the reconstruction of a hand-operated elevator used to hoist animals and gladiators straight into the arena.

The archaeological site near the Trevi Fountain and the Vicolo del Puttarello also deserves attention. Here, you can descend into the Vicus Caprarius, the "Water City," and feel like you are in a historical movie—in a nocturnal scene from a movie set in Rome two thousand years ago. Underneath a cinema, visitors get to see alleys and the remains of several plain but surprisingly well-preserved houses—buildings that were inhabited until the sixth century.

THE POPE'S PARKING LOT

The Vatican preserves very special underground treasures; one is the early Christian necropolis below St. Peter's Basilica with the presumed tomb of Peter the Apostle. Another is the no-less-impressive archaeological area called the Necropolis of the Via Triumphalis. This large underground cemetery is located right beneath the Vatican's multistory car park.

The (required) advance booking for a sightseeing appointment is worth it. It was not until 1956 that the area, which houses burial sites dating from the first century BCE to the fourth century CE, was discovered, excavated, and made accessible via walkways. Visitors get to explore, in a sort of valley basin, surprisingly intact burial sites of diverse sizes. It is certainly one of the most fascinating ancient underground sites in all of Rome.

RIGHT: **ABOVE THE STILL-FUNCTIONING SEWAGE SYSTEM, THE CLOACA MAXIMA, ROME RADIATES IN ALL ITS BEAUTY—DEPICTED IS THE BAROQUE GEM SANTA MARIA DELLA PACE NEAR THE PIAZZA NAVONA.**
OPPOSITE: **SAN VITALE IS ALMOST ENTIRELY COVERED IN FRESCOES.**

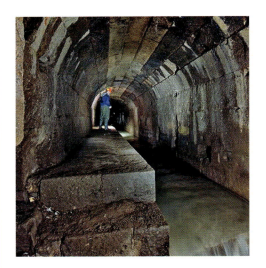

THE OLDEST SEWERAGE SYSTEM IN THE WORLD

In the seventh century BCE, construction began on the Cloaca Maxima, which is the oldest preserved sewage system ever. It was so perfectly designed and put into place that some sections of it are still in operation. And it is even open to visitors—a very unique underground sightseeing thrill in Rome. The descent is down a kind of stone sidewalk along the sewers, past constructions that are more than two thousand years old. On tours, the guides explain exactly (also in English) how the construction of this miles-long sewage system has changed over the centuries. It's an engineering masterpiece that is second to none, but it goes without saying that it does not smell particularly nice down here.

LEARN MORE
Rome: www.turismoroma.it
Roma Sotterranea and Cloaca Maxima: www.romasotterranea.it
Domus Palazzo Valentini: www.palazzovalentini.it
Necropolis of the Via Triumphalis, Vatican: www.museivaticani.va

SUBTERRANEAN LUXURY MANSIONS

The Roman houses of the Celio Hill, the Domus Romane del Celio, mark another rarely visited but extraordinarily fascinating underground location. This ancient city villa dates to the second century CE. Its excellently preserved remains, featuring stucco and murals, rooms and corridors, as well as a once-private thermal bath, were erected along an underground road, where the ruins of an apartment building for the less wealthy can also be visited. The remains of stores on the first floor are easy to identify. Within these two buildings, a new "domus" was erected in the fourth century. It is adorned with magnificent decorations. Later, the Basilica of Saints John and Paul was built on top of these ancient walls.

The Trastevere district also hides an impressive civic building beneath the ground: the Excubitorium, which was not discovered until the 1860s. A sentry post of the ancient Roman city police was housed on these premises. Inscriptions in the walls reveal that the VII. Cohort was stationed here, with barracks in the immediate vicinity. The many examples of antique graffiti on the walls, as well as the well-preserved masonry and an elegant entrance portal, date to the second and third centuries CE.

GOING DEEPER UNDERGROUND

The Basilica di San Vitale is an early Christian church that is not completely underground, but it has been built so far into the ground next to a street that it can only be reached via steeply descending steps. It is located near the central Via Nazionale, often frequented by tourists, yet it is rarely noticed. The church, consecrated in 402 CE, was painted during the Renaissance and baroque periods and houses several art treasures. In late antiquity, it was situated on the Vicus Longus, an ancient road that ran roughly where the Via Nazionale is today. Due to the passage of time and the movement of rubble over the centuries, today San Vitale nestles far below the road, almost underground.

Underneath the surface, Rome offers many surprises. But you should make sure to read up before your trip and book sightseeing tours in advance. The private association Roma Sotterranea – Speleologia per l'Archeologia offers guided underground tours tailored to everyone's taste and fitness levels; there are so many tours, in fact, that you can spend days underground. This company is run by experts and also has tours in its repertoire that require participants to be fairly fit, as you have to crawl and walk bent over for long stretches of time.

Probably the youngest and most modern place of worship underneath Roman soil is the Chiesa di Santa Maria della Pace ai Parioli. It is the main church of the personal prelature of Opus Dei. This odd little church is located behind the façade of a modern building on the Viale Bruno Buozzi. It is generally open to the public from morning to late afternoon. The underground Neo-Romanesque basilica, dug into the ground in the twentieth century and fitted out with columns, frescoes, and artificial light illuminating the faux-old stained-glass windows, gives the impression of being in a regular church aboveground.

PALESTRINA – BUILT WITHIN A TEMPLE
ON HOLY SOIL

There is no other town in Italy that is built within an ancient building. This curious small town demands to be ascended via alleys, steps, and staircases, because the gigantic Roman temple once took over the entire hilltop on which it is situated.

The magic of this place has even featured in literature: German author Thomas Mann and his brother Heinrich stayed in Palestrina for more than a brief visit at the end of the nineteenth century; they spent two entire summers here, in 1895 and 1897.

Heinrich, the older of the two, was so impressed by the—to this day—rather sleepy little town that he immortalized it in his novel *The Little Town* (translated by Winifred Ray). Thomas Mann, for his part, took inspiration from the location for a key scene in his novel *Doctor Faustus*. Palestrina is where the devil meets the novel's protagonist, Doctor Faustus. In his diary entries, Thomas Mann also reveals that he began work on his novel *Buddenbrooks* in Palestrina.

Although the Manns were enticed by Palestrina, few tourists make their way here, despite the fact that the town, with its close to 22,000 inhabits, is located a mere 23 miles (37 kilometers) east of Rome and has a lot to offer. Above all, it features a historical monument that is unique in all of Europe and takes every visitor's breath away.

LIFE AND WORK IN THE TEMPLE

The old town of Palestrina is located right in the middle of a gigantic ancient Roman temple complex. The ruins are so expansive that they can accommodate houses, palaces, and churches. The Santuario, or sanctuary, was dedicated to Fortuna Primigenia and her oracle. Construction on the site began at the beginning of the first century CE, but

the oracle was already worshiped in the first century BCE. The monumental complex towered across seven artificial terraces, which are still largely visible. The lower part of the temple is older than the upper section, where the Fortuna temple was once located.

DANGEROUS ANIMALS AND MONSTERS

The lower part also housed the oracle of the sanctuary, which was in high demand at one time. In one of the grottoes in the lower section was uncovered one of the most impressive mosaics of Roman antiquity: the so-called Palestrina Mosaic or Nile mosaic of Palestrina, which measures almost 20 by 15 feet (6 by 4.5 meters). The magnificent mosaic floor constitutes an imaginative representation of ancient Egypt.

The giant mosaic depicts life-like animals living in the water and on land. The images are exceptionally realistic. It includes snakes and fish, birds in flight, lions, and rare plants and trees, such as the toothbrush tree. Alongside are mythical creatures, such as beasts that are half man, half horse or donkey. The ancient Romans were very familiar with the fauna of central Africa, as demonstrated by these depictions of elephants, gnus, springboks, hippos, crocodiles, guenons, and monkeys. The mosaic was probably completed around the end of the first century BCE. It is considered an artistic highlight of the naturalistic, realist Hellenistic style.

COLOSSAL VIEWS

Palestrina is worth a visit for this mosaic alone, which is second to none even in Italy, with its wealth of Roman art. These days, it is stored in the Palazzo Colonna Barberini. The palazzo is located at

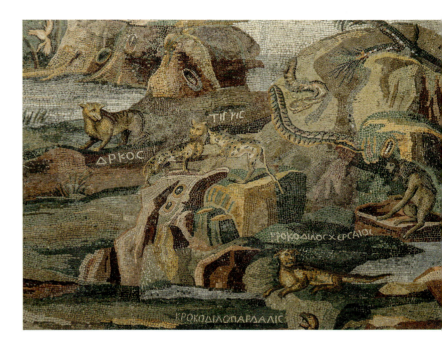

OPPOSITE: **THE VISTA FROM THE "SUMMIT" OF THE ANCIENT TEMPLE DOWN TO THE SMALL TOWN OF PALESTRINA IN THE LATE AFTERNOON.**
BELOW: **ANIMALS ALONG THE COAST: A DETAIL OF THE HUGE MOSAIC IN THE MUSEUM COLONNA BARBERINI.**

the top of the temple complex. Simply stunning is the view from the small piazza, with its fountain over the town built into the temple grounds, the valley, and the mountains in the distance. The National Archaeological Museum of Palestrina, housed in the Palazzo, displays the precious finds from the former temple complex. Besides the mosaic, there are statues, inscriptions, and countless votive offerings from believers.

POLENTA À LA PALESTRINA

Here's an insider tip: go out for lunch in Palestrina! It has some culinary specialties that you simply have to try. For example: chicken ragout served with fettuccini egg pasta. Or homemade polenta with boar ragout. It's a hearty and very savory cuisine! Soups made with chickpeas and broad beans were once pauper dishes, but today, gourmets delight in them. "Giglietti" is a local dessert consisting of biscuits with plenty of eggs and sugar. The wine obviously comes from eastern Lazio, and these full-bodied and straightforward wines perfectly complement the delicacies of this traditional cuisine.

LEARN MORE

Palestrina: www.visitpalestrina.it
Museo Archeologico Nazionale di Palestrina: www.polomusealelazio.beniculturali.it

THIS PAGE: OSTIA ANTICA WAS ONCE THE MOST IMPORTANT PORT OF ANCIENT ITALY—ITS MAGNIFICENT RUINS ARE A TESTAMENT TO IT.
OPPOSITE: AMOR RIDES ON A DOLPHIN ACROSS THE FLOOR OF THE NEPTUNE BATH.

OSTIA ANTICA – POMPEII VIBES

A WALK THROUGH ANTIQUITY

Visitors to this small ruined town will get a fascinating glimpse of what neighboring ancient Rome must have looked like about two thousand years ago. Besides Pompeii, Ostia Antica is the best-preserved ancient Roman city in Italy.

The Via Cristoforo Colombo leads in a straight line from the historical center of Rome to Ostia, this not-very-charming seaside resort. Just to the right, before entering the modern city, however, lies its historical ancestor: Ostia Antica.

Back in the day, until the sixth century CE, the Mediterranean Sea reached up to this point. But over the centuries, the ancient port silted up, and the coast moved further away. Today, the coast and its sandy beaches are located a few miles further west. The ruined town, approximately 14 miles (23 kilometers) from the city center, is easily accessible by car or by local train from Ostia. Sturdy footwear is recommended, as you will cover a good number of miles here.

From the entrance area, you can walk across the main street, as straight as an arrow, directly into the heart of the most important port city of Rome. Ostia Antica was the place of transshipment for all goods that arrived by ship across the sea.

A FORUM WITH A GROUP TOILET

In the wealthy small town, merchants and shipowners were once in charge. And they made sure that the public buildings in Ostia were something to be proud of.

Ostia Antica entertained several temples at once. Three of them, devoted to Minerva, Jupiter, and Juno, were located on the capitol. The Forum, the political center of every Roman city, was rather large at 115 by 52 feet (35 by 16 meters). Unfortunately, only a few building ruins remain, since the Romans and people who lived in the direct vicinity of the ancient town, began in the fifteenth century to use the stones for their new houses.

A public latrine, at least, survived the passage of time. Here, people would sit in rows next to each other, able to have a chat, while running water ensured that the results of the session were quickly flushed away. The group toilet is fairly well preserved.

TEMPLES AND BATHS

The city center is dominated by the Tempio Rotondo, the round temple. The most important building of worship in Ostia, it probably dates back to the beginning of the third century CE. In the early days of Christianity, the Middle Eastern god Mithra was worshipped here as well.

Besides temples reserved for prayer, there were several public baths for relaxation. Their impressive remains demonstrate how lavishly decorated with mosaics, sculptures, and marble they once were. In the second century CE, a Praetorian prefect had the largest of the spas built, featuring black-and-white floor mosaics. Such two-tone mosaics seem to have been en vogue in ancient Ostia, judging by how often you come across them, especially on the sidewalks in front of the city's many former stores.

Of course, Ostia also had an amphitheater. It is so well preserved that open-air events still take place there in the summer—in the evenings when the city ruins are beautifully illuminated. The first theater provided space for three thousand spectators. In the second century, the theater was expanded. Sixteen stores formed part of the complex and are still recognizable today. All brick walls were once richly decorated with marble.

ANCIENT BUSINESS

The Caserma dei Vigili, the firefighters' barracks, can also easily be spotted. For the more than four hundred firefighters, life in the barracks was well organized. A curious feature is the Piazzale delle

THIS PAGE: **THE RECESSES IN THE SACRED BUILDING WERE PROBABLY RESERVED FOR THE VENERATION OF GODS.** *OPPOSITE*: **THE MASK OF HERACLES IN THE AMPHITHEATER HAS RETAINED ITS EXPRESSIVENESS THROUGHOUT THE CENTURIES.**

Corporazioni, the square of the professional guilds. There are seventy small rooms spread out over an area of about 360 by 262 feet (110 by 80 meters). This is where merchants, shipowners, and other businessmen had their seats, as well as people who came here from various parts of the Roman Empire and stayed. Mosaics embedded in the floor outside each of these establishments indicated the respective industry of the owner. Many of the mosaics are still intact. At the former headquarters of the guild of contractors, Caseggiato dei Triclini, a building complex with a courtyard, the stairs leading to the second floor are still visible.

Also fascinating are the former residences of Ostia Antica, such as the once luxuriously decorated House of the Muses, the House of Thunderbolt, and that of Jupiter. The villas and comfortable apartment houses also featured private thermal baths and pools, decorated with mosaics and murals. The mansions with atriums are similar to those of Pompeii. The former apartment houses, which once spread over several floors, were partially reconstructed during the Italian fascist era. They give a really good impression of the modern construction techniques employed for those buildings. The apartments are generously sized, with large windows and hallways from which the individual rooms branched off. There were often stores located on the first floor. The apartment houses also give interesting clues about a social phenomenon; they were mainly erected from the third century onwards, when more and more Romans moved to Ostia to find work and pursue careers.

RELIGIOUS FREEDOM WAS OF PARAMOUNT IMPORTANCE

The fact that Ostia Antica remained a flourishing city until late antiquity, that is, until the end of the Roman Empire in the fifth century, was also due to its cosmopolitan outlook. For a long time, pagan temples, early Christian churches, and Jewish synagogues stood here peacefully side by side.

In 1961, excavations uncovered a large synagogue. It is considered one of the oldest Jewish places of worship outside Palestine. The synagogue must be very old because archaeologists are convinced that it was erected before the destruction of the Temple in Jerusalem—that is, before 70 CE. It features a beautiful, well-preserved depiction of a seven-lamp menorah.

The Museo Archeologico Ostiense is also worth a visit. It houses eleven exhibition halls in a historical building from the fifteenth century that was also built using stone from the ancient city. Some very beautiful finds from Ostia Antica are exhibited here, among them mosaics and murals.

DINING IN NERVI ARCHITECTURE
Take a stroll through Ostia in the morning and then head off to the sea, to elegant Sporting Beach—a chic and clean resort offering great comfort and pretty wooden bathing huts on the beach. In the evening, enjoy a meal on the panoramic terrace of the complex, designed by architect Pier Luigi Nervi in the 1950s. Once upon a time, the stars of Fellini's *La Dolce Vita* dined here. Today, it is a well-kept and not even particularly expensive restaurant known for its fish and seafood dishes. Booking in advance is advisable, to get one of the tables directly by the rail with a view of the beach and the sea.

LEARN MORE
Parco Archeologico di Ostia Antica: www.ostiaantica.beniculturali.it
Sporting Beach: www.sportingbeachroma.com

NINFA – VISITING A MAGIC GARDEN

IN THE REALM OF THE NYMPHS

Wild and tamed nature, alongside the picturesque ruins of a village—all of it is composed as if it were a landscaped garden. Ninfa is an enchanted garden that is second to none. There are 1,300 botanical species in the 20-acre garden (8 hectares).

The first impression is overwhelming; many visitors are speechless and cannot describe the unique beauty of this place. There is a view over the smooth-as-glass water surface of a lake, for example. On the opposite bank—as one scene harmoniously blends into the next, as if composed by an artist—are perfectly straight cypresses and other trees of various shapes, sizes, and colors, all lined up in a row. This green, red, and brown idyll is pierced by the ruins of a medieval castle that seems to emerge from nature as if it were part of the landscape—like a painting, or almost an apparition. The *New York Times* called the Garden of Ninfa one of the most beautiful and romantic spots in the world. And that is not an exaggeration by any means.

The name Ninfa means "nymph." It dates back to Roman antiquity, when a small temple dedicated to the so-called Naiad Nymphs stood here. The mythological female nymphs seem to watch as good spirits over the streams and springs that still exist in the garden. The city that used to be here was destroyed in the fourteenth century. Then, and afterward, the area belonged to the noble family Caetani. They built a family residence here and later designed the Garden of Ninfa.

PLAYING WITH NATURALNESS

In the nineteenth century, the idea of the English landscaped garden became fashionable in Italy as well. This concept champions the notion of a park that is designed in a way that makes it look almost natural. The observer gets the impression that everything here had sprouted on its own accord, without human intervention. In reality, this idea reflects the ideal of a romantic park that is entirely

OPPOSITE: MAN-MADE AND GROWN OVER CENTURIES: NINFA IS A PARADISE GARDEN.
LEFT: THE MEDIEVAL RUINS ADD TO THE OVERALL ROMANTIC IMPRESSION.

created by human hands! In the late nineteenth century, the Caetani family had the surrounding marshes drained and planted beech trees, holm oaks, cypresses, and other trees. While the ruins have been restored, their picturesque ambiance has been preserved.

BIODIVERSITY IN A SMALL SPACE

The 4,447-acre (1,800 hectares) park now houses 1,300 different plants and trees. Nineteen different types of magnolia bloom every year. A visit in spring is simply stunning, when tulip, cherry, and apple trees are in full bloom. Many of them grow directly on the rivers and brooks, which doubles their beautiful appearance, so to speak. Plants and trees native to South America, Africa, and Australia add an exotic touch to the park.

On a walk through the natural landscape, visitors will come across ruins and other historical buildings. They seem to blend into the natural landscape and are completely surrounded by it. There are fourteen churches, remains of the city walls, and the Castello, a castle from the twelfth century, complete with tower and windowless Gothic walls. The main church of Santa Maria Maggiore, from the tenth century, features still recognizable frescoes. There are small ancient bridges throughout the park, one even dating back to Roman times.

Today, the Garden of Ninfa is managed by the WWF and is a national cultural treasure. This paradise is only open to visitors for a few months each year and ideally by prior arrangement. This is mainly to ensure that the many migratory birds from Africa to Northern Europe (and vice versa), which have been stopping over here since time immemorial, can continue to pause here for a rest.

CORI: TEMPLE WITH A VIEW

The village of Cori is a fifteen-minute drive from the Garden of Ninfa and extends up the Monti Lepini. The miniature town had already sported a town wall in the fifth century BCE. Within the wall are dark and narrow alleys with steps and ramps, simple small residential houses, and the curious and picturesque Via del Porticato, a street almost completely covered by medieval buildings. From the impressive remains of the Temple of Hercules outside the city walls, eight elegant Doric columns remain erect. The panoramic view from the temple into the valley is astounding. A local culinary specialty is "Prosciutto di Cori"; after having been matured for sixteen months, the local ham is wrapped in herbs and cooked in local white wine. It tastes fantastic!

LEARN MORE
Giardino di Ninfa: www.giardinodininfa.eu
Cori: www.scoprirecori.it

AN EVENING STROLL BY THE SEA—IN SOUTHERN ITALY, THAT IS POSSIBLE ALMOST ALL YEAR ROUND.

SOUTHERN ITALY
Art Treasures and Natural Marvels

THIS PAGE: THE TERM "STAIRCASE" DOES NOT QUITE CUT IT. RATHER, IT IS A "GALA STAIRWELL" WITH BAROQUE SPLENDOR. *OPPOSITE*: HUGE, RECTANGULAR, AND A LITTLE IMPOSING: THE ROYAL PALACE OF CASERTA.

CASERTA – THE LARGEST CASTLE IN THE WORLD
CHARMING MEGALOMANIA

An enormous castle where magnificent balls were held, with a Court Theater that put on the most beautiful operas by the Neapolitan School: the magnificent palace of Caserta was meant to rival the French Sun King's Versailles.

The castle boasts 1,200 rooms and 1,742 windows . . . and look at those dimensions! The longest side of the almost-square building measures 817 feet (249 meters). The palazzo is almost 125 feet (38 meters) tall. There are 1,026 chimneys and thirty-four staircases. The most impressive of these is 60 feet (18.5 meters) wide, 47.5 feet (14.5 meters) high, and comprises 117 steps. The palace has four courtyards, each of which is 40,900 square feet (3,800 square meters) in size. Some of the walls are 18 feet (5.5 meters) thick. The total area of the building occupies an incredible 505,900 square feet (47,000 square meters). Reggia di Caserta is the largest royal palace in the world. The complex, along with its magnificent park, was named a UNESCO World Heritage Site in 1997.

BIGGER, MORE BEAUTIFUL, MORE BOMBASTIC

It was Charles of Bourbon—who was Duke of Parma and Piacenza until 1735 and King of Naples and

Sicily until 1759, before he became the Spanish regent and representative of the Italian Bourbons—who wanted to prove to his French relatives, especially Louis XIV, that he could have an even larger castle built than the Palace of Versailles.

Work on the mega palace began in 1752. It was inaugurated in 1774 but only completed in 1845, as a plain building with cool elegance and few decorative elements on the outside. Even during Charles of Bourbon's time did detractors call the Palace of Caserta the "Grand Italian Barracks." Reggia di Caserta is the work of two masters of Italian neoclassical architecture: Luigi and Carlo Vanvitelli. The king's explicit order to the father-and-son team was not just to design a royal palace but to build the most magnificent royal residence that ever was. "No scrimping and much spending" seemed to be his motto.

A RIVAL TO VERSAILLES

Although several rooms have been modified and renovated over the past two centuries, many of the original furniture has been preserved. Instead of the lavish baroque and abundant Rococo designs characteristic of Versailles, cool elegance dominates this space. The castle is a dream of neoclassicism that has come to life.

To get to the main stairwell, you have to cross an octagonal vestibule supported by twenty Doric columns. Once the gigantic staircase opens up in front of you, you cannot help but marvel at it, rendered speechless. From here, you head directly to the palace chapel and the so-called state rooms, where the king and his family would present themselves to the court.

A sequence of large halls leads to the royal apartments. The Old Apartment consists of eleven halls that reflect the owners' taste. The king's

LEFT: **THE PALACE GLEAMS IN THE DISTANCE. THE GARDEN COMPRISES 247 ACRES (100 HECTARES) INTERSPERSED WITH WATER FEATURES SUCH AS THIS VENUS FOUNTAIN.** *ABOVE*: **THE COURT THEATER STILL EXISTS JUST AS IT DID IN THE EIGHTEENTH CENTURY.**

study has an Asian look, and the bathroom includes all the modern conveniences of the late eighteenth century. The library of Queen Maria Carolina, the wife of Charles's heir to the throne, King Ferdinand, is still intact, including its approximately 12,000 books. Paintings by Italian and Dutch masters adorn the walls.

The New Apartment, which was only completed in 1845, after almost forty years of construction, includes the Throne Room. With its 44 by 118 feet (13.5 by 36 meters), the hall is simply enormous and much more imposing than the Southern Italian kings' actual political influence in Europe at that time. The Court Theater, which has also been completely preserved, has a unique appeal. It can accommodate 450 spectators and has fantastic acoustics. At the end of the eighteenth century, operas by Giovanni Paisiello and Domenico Cimarosa, the two musical stars of the Neapolitan School, were performed here.

A MANGER OF STATURE

One of the exceptional highlights of Reggia di Caserta is the Presepe Reale, the Royal Manger. It occupies 430 square feet (40 square meters). More than 1,200 figures populate the urban landscape of this Nativity scene, which is an almost identical replica of a town in the middle of the eighteenth century, with its varied buildings and churches, alleys and squares, and stores and markets. The actual biblical events almost go unnoticed in this stage set.

Part of the palace complex is a 296-acre park (120 hectares), 1.8 miles (3 kilometers) in length. It is based on two styles. Around the Fontana dei Delfini, whose basin is 1,542 by 88.5 feet (470 by 27 meters), the park follows the classical Italian rules of a geometrical garden layout. The other part of the park corresponds to a landscape garden in the style that has been en vogue in England since the late eighteenth century.

CLEVER WATER FEATURES

Fountains and wells enliven the park, which is crisscrossed by several paths and in part decorated with sculptures that are several feet tall. The Fontana di Cerere is a magnificent water feature with seven small cascades and sculptures depicting river gods. An abundance of water is pumped to Caserta via an aqueduct that extends over a distance of 25.5 miles (41 kilometers) and bridges

SILK AND SOCIAL BENEFITS

In 1773, King Ferdinand IV created a private refuge in San Leucio, not far from the palace. When his son died of the plague shortly afterward, the king converted this retreat into one of the first European social projects: a place where the poor could live and work in a modern and clean environment. One of the best silk factories in Europe was set up, complete with the most modern machines. For the children of these workers, schooling was compulsory and free of charge. All workers enjoyed rights and social benefits that were unique for their time. This silk colony, with its restored residential buildings and workplaces, is now a UNESCO World Heritage Site. Silk has been produced here again for the past several years and is sold on site.

LEARN MORE

Caserta: www.casertaturismo.it
Reggia di Caserta: www.reggiadicaserta.beniculturali.it
San Leucio: www.sanleucio.it

valleys at a height of up to 180 feet (55 meters). It's truly a feat of civil engineering!

The Italian Bourbons did not live in their palace for very long. In 1806, conquering Napoleon took it from them, and the Southern Italian king was not able to use it again until 1815. The year 1860 brought an end to the Bourbon reign altogether. As part of a newly united Italy, the entire south fell to the Piedmontese kings. Reggia di Caserta was completely restored only in recent years and dazzles visitors again in its former, elegant splendor.

TRANI – CATHEDRAL BY THE SEA

UNADULTERATED ROMANESQUE CULTURE

In this small seaside town, one of the most impressive churches in Southern Italy towers in direct proximity to the Adriatic Sea. Despite having been exposed to wind and weather for more than 800 years, it has lost none of its charm.

San Nicola Pellegrino stands on the piazza, isolated and alone, thanks to an intervention by town planners in the 1950s. This was a wise move, because it underlines the impression of a church bulwark directly by the sea. This way, the beauty of this medieval building is visible from all sides. The Trani Cathedral in Puglia was built on the ruins of an early Christian complex dating back to the fifth century. Today's church is a work of the eleventh to thirteenth centuries and constitutes one of the most fascinating examples of Romanesque architecture in Italy.

CHURCH BELOW, CHURCH ABOVE

It is a double church with a crypt. Strangely, visitors enter it via a stairway. This staircase had become necessary because one church towers over another here—similar to the Umbrian Assisi, which also features a lower and an upper church.

Both churches are very light in color due to the local stone that was used for their construction. Even the salty air of the Adriatic Sea has no adverse effect on this weather-resistant stone with its reddish tint. The façades feature many Romanesque works of art, such as depictions of the battle of a lion, as part of a group of sculptures at the entrance. The bronze portal was created in 1175 by a local artist. The windows are framed with columns and sculptures, and the façades are decorated with ornamental bands.

The back of the cathedral makes it obvious how far the church sticks into the sky. The apse in the center extends all the way to the roof of the transept. Curiously, the campanile stands atop the high arch of a passageway.

OPPOSITE: **THE ROMANESQUE CATHEDRAL TOWERS OVER THE COAST LIKE A FORTRESS BY THE SEA.** *LEFT:* **FRESH DAILY AND STRAIGHT FROM THE SEA: FISH IN THE MARKET OF TRANI.**

A SHRINE BELOW SEA LEVEL

The interior of San Nicola Pellegrino is enormous. And yet, it hides an oddity: the lower level of the interior, which includes the tomb of Saint Leucius, a bishop who died in the third century and whose earthly remains were venerated until the ninth, is located below the sea level of the Adriatic. Double columns, arcades, galleries, and mullioned windows subdivide the interior walls. The church was initially decorated with frescoes, but these have all but completely faded. Later additions, such as those made in the baroque era, have disappeared as well. Thus, the interior exudes the severe yet alluring elegance of an unadulterated Romanesque church.

The fact that the small town of Trani could afford such an imposing church has to do with the Normans, the descendants of the Vikings. They conquered Southern Italy at the beginning of the eleventh century. Back then, the city was one of the most important ports of Christian Europe for its trade with the Orient. Mainly thanks to the Crusaders, local trade flourished in the twelfth and thirteenth centuries.

Nowadays, Trani is a sleepy town, where nothing much happens, but it does offer a charming historical town center. The old buildings were all built using local Trani stone—for example, the Castello Svevo belonging to the Holy Roman Emperor Frederick II and the Palazzo Caccetta from the fifteenth century, as well as the Church of Ognissanti, a former hospice of the Knights Templars dating back to the thirteenth century.

Trani had a lively Jewish community until the Spaniards took over the reins of Southern Italy in the sixteenth century. The Scolanova Synagogue bears witness to this. The Spanish converted it into a church, but in 2005 it was rededicated as a temple for the Jewish population once again.

CASTEL DEL MONTE – THE DREAM OF THE HOUSE OF HOHENSTAUFEN

About a half-hour drive from Trani, one of Italy's most mysterious buildings towers atop a mountain. Is it a hunting lodge? Or a place for mystical rites? Frederick II, of the Hohenstaufen dynasty, had this castle built in the middle of the thirteenth century—and left the legacy of a unique building. The walls above the octagonal floor plan are 82 feet (25 meters) high, while the towers rise to 85 feet (26 meters). Each of the sides measures 54 feet (16.5 meters) in length. The courtyard is octagonal as well. The design of the rooms gives almost no indication whatsoever as to the function of the building. Although it looks like a fortress, the Castel was not a defensive structure, because there is no moat nor are there any embrasures. To this day, this remote place is shrouded in secrecy.

LEARN MORE
Trani: www.viaggiareinpuglia.it
Castel del Monte: www.casteldelmonte.beniculturali.it

NAPLES – ITALY'S MOST FASCINATING CITY

QUEEN OF THE SOUTH

Greeks, Romans, Goths, Spaniards, and Bourbons, plus a splash of Arab influences and customs dating back to pagan antiquity: Naples has got a little bit of everything . . . and sometimes a little too much of it. It is Italy's busiest, craziest, and most fascinating city.

How should you visit this city? What comes to mind when you think of Naples? Some people think of the mafia, which is called the Camorra here, and which plies its dreadful trade almost everywhere, even though you may not notice it. At the mention of Naples, music lovers may think of the Teatro San Carlo, one of the largest and most beautiful opera houses in Europe, dating to the eighteenth century. Others may think of the ancient treasures in the National Archaeological Museum. Most foreigners will certainly think of pizza, which—according to the Neapolitans—was "invented" in the alleys of the old town many centuries ago. Pizza is more delicious here than anywhere else.

If you want to approach the city cautiously and would like to return to a peaceful place—away from the hustle and bustle—after your explorations, book a hotel above the old town in the hilltop district of Vomero. But if you want to be right where it's at, consider staying in the Spanish Quarter, the "Quartieri Spagnoli," or at the Piazza del Plebiscito.

THIS PAGE: GAMBRINUS, THE CITY'S FINEST COFFEE HOUSE, IS AN ESSENTIAL PART OF NAPLES. *OPPOSITE:* SO ARE ARE THE ELEGANT BOULEVARDS, PALACES, AND MUSEUMS REPLETE WITH ART.

Naples must be explored on foot; it is the only way to understand how many different facets this city has to offer—ranging from different eras and both above and below ground.

LIBERAL ANTIQUITY

The National Archaeological Museum provides insights into ancient Naples. It has one of the world's most important collections of ancient art, sculptures, and furnishings from ancient Greek and Roman villas, as well as the so-called Gabinetto Segreto, the "Secret Cabinet": a room with an astonishing collection of erotic art. This museum also exhibits one of the most impressive mosaics of antiquity. The unknown artist used more than one and a half million mosaic pieces to depict a battle led by Alexander the Great on an area of almost 20 by 10 feet (6 by 3 meters). However, whether this unique work of art really dates to the fourth century BCE remains disputed.

The elegant Via Toledo, which travels past one former noble palace after another, leads straight to the Royal Palace, the Palazzo Reale. The large palace complex in the style of the eighteenth century offers magnificently restored interiors within the royal apartments. Next to the Royal Palace is the impressive late baroque Teatro di San Carlo opera house. Opposite, Gran Caffè Gambrinus invites visitors to take a break. It is one of the oldest and best-preserved coffee houses in Italy, with elegant nineteenth-century furniture and genuine Neapolitan treats.

Behind the opera house is Castel Nuovo, one of Italy's most famous fortresses from the late Middle Ages and the early Renaissance. To the north of the fortification lies the maze of streets and alleyways of the old town. It is home to unique buildings, including churches that are not only places of worship but also art galleries, such as Santa Chiara, built in the fourteenth century. The

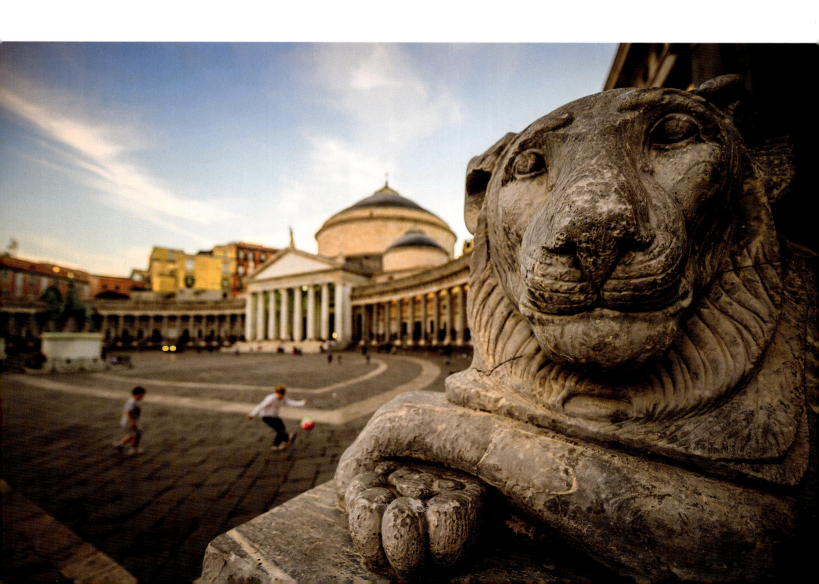

interior of this church is as spacious as a hangar. Destroyed in World War II by US shelling, the mighty church was faithfully reconstructed in the southern French Gothic style. The cloisters are particularly beautiful, decorated with painted majolica tiles.

The Jesuit Gesù Nuovo Church hides an abundance of baroque art behind a façade of diamond projections. The almost whimsically elaborate decoration clearly shows that Naples was part of the Spanish Empire for a long time; Spanish baroque is characterized by an abundance of embellishments.

VEILED CHRIST

The late medieval painter Pietro Cavallini created the magnificent murals in the church of San Domenico Maggiore in the early fourteenth century. Ten Spanish rulers are buried in the sacristy. Not far from here, you can visit one of the most elaborate and enchanting sculptures of Italian baroque in the Sansevero Chapel. Prince Raimondo di Sangro was a mystic, an alchemist, an author, and one of the best-known thinkers of the European Enlightenment. He commissioned the sculptor Giuseppe Sanmartino to produce a piece that, after its completion in 1753, would become well-known far beyond Italy. It shows a life-sized man stretched out on a kind of bed. His athletic marble body is covered with a cloth that looks true to life. It gives the impression of a living person lying under an almost transparent veil.

From the chapel, it is not far to Naples' Christmas street, the Via San Gregorio Armeno. Throughout the year, countless workshops produce Nativity scenes, complete with manger and statuettes. From small stables to extensive Nativity scenes, this traditional Neapolitan craft goes back to the seventeenth century.

THE HEART OF THE OLD TOWN

The Neapolitan worship of Saint Gennaro, or Saint Januarius, originated in late antiquity. A vial of the dried blood of the city's patron saint, who died in 305 CE, is kept in Naples Cathedral. This relic is extremely important to many of the city's 970,000 inhabitants. If, at the annual ceremonies conducted by the bishop, Saint Januarius's blood fails to liquefy, it predicts a bad prognosis for the near future. On the other hand, if the blood does become liquid,

OPPOSITE: **PIAZZA POLITEAMA MARKS THE CENTER OF THE OLD TOWN, RIGHT NEXT TO THE ROYAL PALACE.** *TOP*: **THE SPANISH QUARTER IS FAMOUS FOR ITS PERFECTLY STRAIGHT NARROW ALLEYS.** *BOTTOM*: **A HISTORIC STEEL STRUCTURE WITH GLASS DOMES SPANS THE SPACIOUS GALLERIA UMBERTO I.**

BELOW: SOME TRADITIONAL NATIVITY STATUETTES IN THE VIA SAN GREGORIO ARMENO VERGE ON KITSCH. *RIGHT*: THE TEATRO SAN CARLO OPERA HOUSE IS ONE OF THE LARGEST AND OLDEST IN THE WORLD.

Naples is safe from disaster. The cathedral's treasure is one of the wealthiest in the world and is definitely worth a visit. It's a triumph of Neapolitan baroque art and gold work, above all.

The infamous painter Caravaggio also lived in Naples for a while. He created a magnificent altarpiece for the church of Pio Monte della Misericordia that is still venerated by Neapolitans today.

The traditional heart of Naples still beats in the Quartieri Spagnoli district, the area west of the Via Toledo. You should only walk around the Spanish Quarter during the day, though—it can get dangerous after dark. You should be careful during the day as well, but if you behave and dress inconspicuously, you should have nothing to worry about. The Spanish Quarter is a succession of quaint artisan shops, inviting cake shops, small pizzerias, and apartments, the so-called "bassi," which are located a couple of steps below street level. This district is home to the Fondazione Cappella dei Turchini, a music school that teaches children and adolescents the music of the Neapolitan baroque. They regularly put on classical concerts.

FANTASTIC VIEWS

Behind the Spanish Quarter rises Vomero, both a hill and a town within the city, which features a much calmer atmosphere. Visitors to Naples will find several addresses worth visiting here. The National Museum of Ceramics is perhaps the most important Italian pottery museum, exhibiting beautiful objects from the great European porcelain manufacturers. From the terraces of the Certosa di San Martino, a huge monastery complex, you can enjoy a view beyond compare of Naples, the Gulf, the islands, and Mount Vesuvius. The church is a treasure trove of sacred art from the Renaissance and the baroque era. The monastery is home to the National Museum of San Martino, which owns the best collection of historical Nativity scenes

THE COURTYARD OF THE SANTA CHIARA CLOISTERS IS DECORATED WITH HAND-PAINTED TILES FROM THE EIGHTEENTH CENTURY.

worldwide, including the the eighteenth-century Presepe Cuciniello, which is populated with numerous figures of people and animals.

Above the old town, the Bourbons had another palace built. Nowadays, the Palazzo Reale di Capodimonte presents one of the most impressive collections of paintings in Europe. The most important works here were created by the great masters of Italian painting: Caravaggio, Raphael, Andrea Mantegna, Filippo Lippi, Michelangelo, and others. You should give yourself plenty of time here in order to appreciate all the treasures.

SUBTERRANEAN NAPLES

In addition to Naples aboveground, there is also an underground city, which is immensely fascinating. Guided tours open up the mysterious world that goes as far back as Greek antiquity. This world lies at a depth of up to 131 feet (40 meters), where the first inhabitants of Naples settled about 2,500 years ago. The tour follows along corridors—some narrow, others wide—and through halls and series of rooms, as well as past the remains of a Greek-Roman theater.

Catacombs are also a part of Naples' underworld. The most impressive of these, the Catacombs of San Gennaro, date back to the third century CE. This is also where you'll find the oldest portrait of the city's patron saint, from the fifth century. Murals, multistory tombs, corridors for corpses, and large halls alternate. This catacomb can be reached from the district of Sanità. Like the Spanish Quarter, this neighborhood is considered very traditional as well. Although many of the former palazzi seem a bit dilapidated today, Sanità is one of the most beautiful places in Naples, since it is one of the most authentic: a neighborhood full of life and impressions.

WHERE THE EARTH IS STEAMING

By metro from the city center of Naples, it takes about one hour to reach the Campi Flegrei, the Phlegraean Fields. They form the surface of a super volcano deep underground, which, if it were ever to erupt, would bury Europe under a blanket of ash for a long time. These volcanic fields consist of Solfatara craters, sulfur fumaroles, which can be visited near Pozzuoli. The crater, with a diameter of almost 2,625 feet (800 meters), is surrounded on three sides by steep walls. The smell is barbaric since hot sulfur and other gases escape from countless fumaroles at a temperature of 392 degrees Fahrenheit (200 degrees Celsius). The ground rises and drops imperceptibly to humans, but measuring instruments attest that it has been rising steadily for several years and that the volcano could eventually erupt.

LEARN MORE
Naples: www.visit-napoli.com
National Archaeological Museum: www.museoarcheologiconapoli.com
Subterranean Naples: www.napolisotterranea.org
Pozzuoli, Solfatara crater: www.solfatara.it

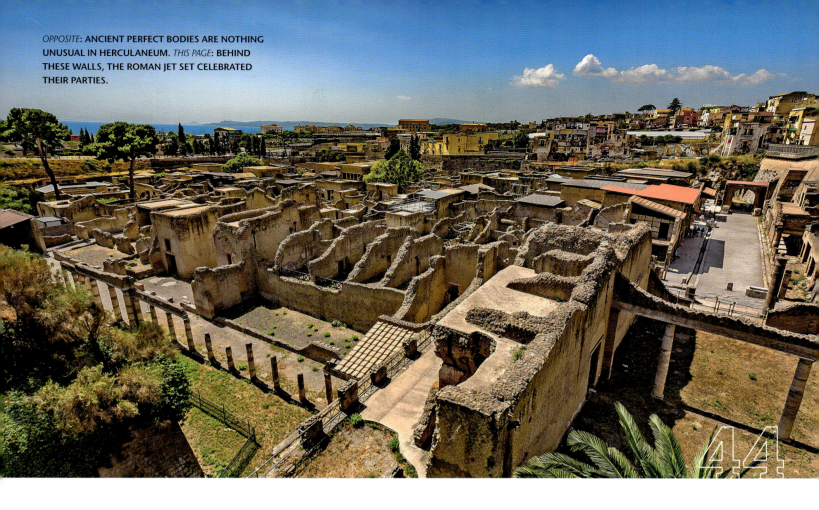

OPPOSITE: ANCIENT PERFECT BODIES ARE NOTHING UNUSUAL IN HERCULANEUM. *THIS PAGE:* BEHIND THESE WALLS, THE ROMAN JET SET CELEBRATED THEIR PARTIES.

HERCULANEUM – POMPEII IN MINIATURE
A BRIEF VISIT TO YESTERYEAR

Almost every tourist in Italy has heard of Pompeii. But although it was only a third of the size of its famous neighbor, Herculaneum, which was likewise buried under volcanic ash in 79 CE, has beautiful villas to offer. After all, the ancient city was considered the place to be for the Roman elite.

A Frenchman was the first to organize a systematic dig under the small town of Resina, now called Ercolano, at his own expense. Emmanuel Maurice, Duke of Elbeuf, was a commander in the Austrian army at the court of the Holy Roman Emperor at Naples. He was fascinated by antiquity, and since he had heard of locals who kept finding ancient sculptures or fragments thereof in the ground around Resina during construction work, he put two and two together. The aristocrat was convinced that something must be hidden underneath these buildings, so he sponsored the excavation of underground tunnels. His discovery caused a stir throughout Europe. The duke gifted some of the discovered works of art to the Austrian field marshal Prince Eugene of Savoy in Vienna, which is how the myth of Herculaneum became known throughout Europe.

THE KING ORDERS THE DIG
His interest piqued, the South Italian Bourbon king Charles VII also commissioned excavations here beginning in the late 1730s. During these digs, an inscription was uncovered that clearly proved to the experts at the time that Resina had been built atop an ancient city. The inscription read "Theatrum Herculanense," and where there was an ancient theater, an ancient city could not be far

away. But it was hidden underneath a layer of ash that was 39 to 82 feet thick (12 to 25 meters).

In the deep shafts and galleries, the experts made one discovery after another. When the surprisingly well-preserved remains of a luxurious villa were uncovered in 1750, a real excavating frenzy set in. This luxury mansion, the Villa of the Papyri, concealed a very special treasure that has not been completely uncovered to this day because it is extremely delicate: the library, which contains more than 1,800 charred remains of papyrus scrolls. This specialist library—which US billionaire J. Paul Getty had faithfully reproduced in Los Angeles—features scriptures by Greek thinkers, some of them unique to it. Using highly sensitive technology, the remains have been researched for years to decipher the remaining scrolls—a Herculean task, quite literally.

The early excavations only made gradual progress and were not coordinated or controlled by the state, which meant that many ancient works of art were sold abroad. Only since 1924, and thanks to Benito Mussolini's enthusiasm for antiquity, did the systematic and ongoing archaeological excavation work in Herculaneum begin. In order to bring this small town back to light on a grand scale, 22 acres (9 hectares) of urban land were expropriated, and many houses had to be demolished. Today it is clear that the ancient city reaches deep below the present-day town.

LIFESTYLES OF THE RICH AND FAMOUS

In contrast with expansive Pompeii, which takes a lot of time to visit, Herculaneum seems like a distillation. It offers visitors several excellently preserved private villas within the ancient center and beyond, toward the sea. The works of art are a testament to the fact that the inhabitants of these buildings were fairly wealthy; these are now located in the National Archaeological Museum of Naples.

The so-called Casa Sannitica from the second century BCE is particularly impressive. The individual rooms can be easily identified, even those on the second floor, as can the wall decorations. The

LEFT: **THE RECONSTRUCTED CASA A GRATICCIO IS AN ANTIQUE HALF-TIMBERED HOUSE.** *ABOVE*: **THE FLOORS OF THE WOMEN'S AND MEN'S THERMAL BATHS ARE CLAD WITH MOSAICS.** *OPPOSITE*: **ENTIRE ROWS OF HOUSES HAVE BEEN PRESERVED IN HERCULANEUM.**

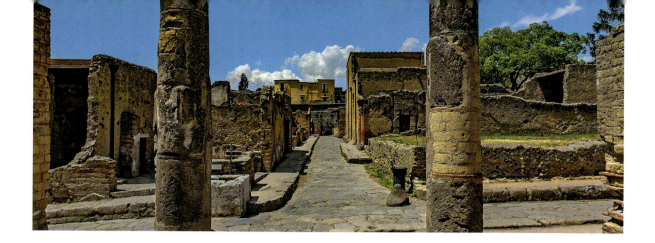

structure of the villa is so well preserved that it is hard to believe that it was buried for about two thousand years. Visitors can even make out the outlines of the gardens. The Casa dell'Atrio a Mosaico offered about 12,917 square feet (1,200 square meters) of living space. Mosaics cover much of the floors. Large-scale frescoes decorate its walls.

FEUDAL BATHS

The Suburban Baths, a multistory building in the Herculaneum docklands, dating back to the first century CE, is particularly beautiful and unique, even by Italian standards. It gives an excellent impression of how the ancient Romans were enjoying themselves in the public baths. Columns support the ceiling arches, and the masonry remains almost intact—as is the erotic graffiti on some walls, because we may not forget that a thermal bath was also a place of sexual encounters where women and boys offered their services. The changing room, covered by an arched ceiling, extends along the walls and is of gigantic proportions. The mosaic floors of the so-called apodyterium, or "waiting room," depict marine gods and creatures, such as octopuses, and have been completely preserved. The Casa di Nettuno e Anfitrite features beautiful multicolored wall mosaics in the room where the proud owners probably held their sumptuous evening banquets.

The freedman Q. Granius Verus, who made a fortune after he gained his freedom, had a villa built here in the first century CE that is now called Casa dei Cervi. This large complex once opened up to the sea along the length of one side. Mosaic floors and the remains of elegant murals and wall mosaics are still visible. Fascinating wall frescoes depict scenes of everyday life.

Walking through ancient Herculaneum, you will also notice the Casa a Graticcio, a kind of antique half-timbered house built using stone and timber. The entire second floor has been preserved. Despite having mentioned these important points of interest, visitors are encouraged to let themselves drift through Herculaneum. Even on a relaxing stroll, you will get to see much more at once here than in its more famous twin town of Pompeii.

MOUNT VESUVIUS – CLIMBING THE "EVIL MOUNTAIN"

It became legendary when it erupted in 79 CE. Although Mount Vesuvius, at 3,714 feet (1,132 meters), is the most dangerous still-active volcano in Europe, conquering it is possible and recommended. Simply stunning is the view from the summit into the volcano and out onto the Gulf of Naples with the islands of Capri and Ischia. The first 3,280 feet (1,000 meters) or so of the ascent are done by car or a regular bus. A shuttle bus takes visitors even closer to the summit. From there, it is only a twenty-minute walk to the crater's edge. Plan this trip for a day with good visibility. But do take a jacket with you, because it can get cool at the summit, even in summer!

LEARN MORE
Parco Archeologico di Ercolano: www.ercolano.beniculturali.it
Mount Vesuvius: www.visitpompeiivesuvius.com

PAESTUM – EXQUISITE DORIC TEMPLES

GREEK VIBES

To see some of the most beautiful temples of ancient Greece, you only have to hop on the local train from Salerno. Two huge temples rise from the meadow near Paestum, not far from the sea.

The ancient Greeks were a traveling and conquering bunch. No wonder, then, that from the eighth century BCE, they also settled in Sicily, in today's Puglia and Calabria, where they founded trading towns. They ventured as far as the northern part of Southern Italy, to the present-day region of Campania, and built their temples in the flat hinterland of the coast. Cilento is a fertile area, where people cultivate the land. Just like the Greeks once did.

THREE IMPRESSIVE TEMPLES

The Greeks called today's Paestum "Poseidonia." In the fifth century BCE, the small town was a flourishing trading post. And the temples that the people built were clearly designed to bear witness to this prosperity; they are temples of the size, elegance, and beauty usually only found in Greece or, at most, in southern Sicily near Agrigento.

Poseidonia, which the Romans later renamed Paestum, is still partly surrounded by a wall of almost 2.8 miles (4.5 kilometers). Visitors enter the temple complex along the former Via Sacra, the "Holy Road."

The first Temple of Hera, the "Basilica," was built between 550 and 450 BCE in the elegant Doric style. A total of thirty-eight columns are part of it—columns that, upon closer inspection, reveal a slightly domed center, which is a typical feature of the Doric order.

The Temple of Neptune is considered one of the best-preserved masterpieces of the classical Greek period. It was probably built around 460 BCE. Also built in the Doric style, it features six columns at the front and back, and fourteen along each of the sides. It is an imposing

OPPOSITE: **THE GREEK TEMPLES LOOK PARTICULARLY ENCHANTING AT SUNSET.**
LEFT: **THE DIVER IS CONSIDERED ONE OF THE MOST FAMOUS GREEK FRESCOES IN ITALY.**

temple—the largest of the ancient city—that presents itself as uncommonly intact to present-day visitors, and it is considered to be one of the most impressive Greek buildings in the whole Mediterranean region.

The much smaller Temple of Athena dates from the same period. The decorative elements embellishing the architrave and other components above the columns are easily recognizable. The Romans, who conquered the city in the third century BCE, left behind an amphitheater, the city wall, four large gates, and the Comitium, where the free citizens gathered. The fact that all three temples of Paestum have remained intact is because after the fall of the Roman Empire and until well into the nineteenth century, they had remained more or less forgotten, and only individual travelers here and there took an interest in them.

STARK-NAKED DIVER

The Paestum archaeological park boasts a worthwhile museum. On display are murals from the tombs, including one that has become world-famous: it depicts an athletic, stark-naked man jumping from a tower into the water. This representation has been interpreted as a metaphor for the transition from life to the realm of the dead.

The thirty-three well-preserved metopes from the sixth century BCE are very beautiful. These are reliefs on sections of the frieze above the Doric columns. German poet Johann Wolfgang von Goethe must have regarded these mythical scenes as well when he visited the temples on March 23, 1787, as he noted in his *Italian Journey*.

BELLA NATURA!

Less than an hour's drive north of the temples, near Vietri sul Mare, is the start of one of the most beautiful and most picturesque coastlines in Italy: the Amalfi Coast. The coastline boasts legendary towns such as Maiori; Ravello, where Richard Wagner was inspired for his opera *Parsifal*; Amalfi, with its black-and-white striped cathedral from the Middle Ages; and Positano, whose white houses seem to grow upwards along the coastal mountains like in an amphitheater. The road, with its countless viewpoints, leads on to Sorrento, where ferries take off for Capri. A tour around the peninsula can be comfortably done in two days.

LEARN MORE
Paestum: www.paestum.it
Paestum Tempel: www.museopaestum.beniculturali.it

46

MATERA – A COZY CAVE SYSTEM

SENSATIONAL ROCKS

For thousands of years, people lived here in a unique setting—in a city carved into the ground. Matera, which still uses the water pipe system designed back then, is one of the most unusual places in all of Italy.

When you arrive in Matera, in Southern Italian Basilicata, a region little visited by tourists, you don't yet know what awaits you. The old center of this 60,000-inhabitant town is quite charming. But it is when you climb up to one of the terraces at a piazza and look down at the Sassi districts that you are truly rendered speechless. You will perceive something completely new and unusual, one of its kind in Europe. In the Paleolithic period, people began to carve out the rock. They first dug out plain caves and later expanded them into habitable and quite comfortable dwellings. This is how, in the course of the millennia, the two so-called Sassi di Matera districts were born: Sasso Caveoso and Sasso Barisano. They are the true historical and ancient center of Matera. The Sassi of Matera are among the longest inhabited places in the world.

COMFORTABLE GROTTO

Along a slope down into the canyon-like valley of the Gravina River, a dense network of alleys, buildings, and churches grew bit by bit in the karst landscape. It was relatively easy to work the soft sandstone and tuff to carve out grottoes and other hollows. Initially, only the plain grottoes were inhabited. But since the rock was easy to handle and shape, people expanded these initial accommodations and enlarged them. Proper apartments were built into the rock, complete

with corridors and a series of rooms, both with and without windows.

Later, people quarried entire blocks of stone from the mountain to use as a building material for further dwellings. The Sassi developed into a densely populated area, where one house was piled on top of another. The result of this curious construction technique is a dense side-by-side and topsy-turvy arrangement in the rock and a nested network of buildings aboveground, including alleys and squares and impressive rock-hewn churches, which are a one-off—even in Italy. It's no wonder, then, that the Sassi of Matera are part of the UNESCO World Heritage List of Humanity. When darkness falls and the first lights are switched on, the scenery gives the impression of a huge Nativity scene.

A WALK ACROSS THE ROOFTOPS

The "layering" of the many buildings means that visitors on a tour through Sassi will necessarily walk across the roofs of some of these living quarters. High above the Sassi district towers the silhouette of the Cathedral of Matera, an elegant and imposing Romanesque church dating from the thirteenth century. Inside, baroque sets the scene, with a Nativity scene from 1534 as its center point.

A walk along the level, pedestrianized streets Via del Duomo, Via delle Beccherie, Via del Corso, and Via Lucana is a must. The Via Fiorentini goes straight through Sasso Barisano district. The Via Madonna delle Virtù offers a view of both Sassi. They were inhabited until the 1960s. Then, politicians in Rome put an end to this ancient style of living, referencing the unhealthy living conditions in these caves. Residents were forced to move into modern apartment houses, and the Sassi fell into disrepair.

OPPOSITE: **LIVING AND WORKING IN CAVES—PEOPLE HAVE DONE SO IN MATERA FOR THOUSANDS OF YEARS.** *BELOW*: **SOME OF THE SASSI CAVES ARE OPEN TO VISITORS TO SPEND THE NIGHT.**

Later, they were rediscovered and painstakingly restored. Thanks to the age-old, sophisticated irrigation system that supplies all homes with fresh water via canals, channels, pipes, and tubes in an elaborate way, people can now live here again. You can try it yourself by staying in one of the charming hotels!

SACRED ROCKS

Among Matera's special attractions are its unusual rock-hewn churches. They combine the bare and barren charm of the karst landscape with the artistry of the architects who built these small houses of worship between the eighth and thirteenth centuries. Santa Maria della Palomba is particularly fascinating. It sits right above the Gravina River. (It's a must for visitors to not be prone to a fear of heights.) Behind its Romanesque façade, part of the fresco-decorated interior was carved out of the rock. Once you make your way here, we recommend a stroll to Belvedere Murgia Timone, which is less than a ten-minute walk away. From the panorama viewpoint, all sights present themselves to you in one go: Matera, the Sassi districts, the cathedral, and Castello Tramontano.

LEARN MORE
Matera: www.visitmatera.it
Sassi di Matera: www.sassidimatera.it

MARTINA FRANCA – A STYLISH OLD TOWN

UNDER THE PUGLIAN SKIES

This small town is an architect's dream. Or it appears like a large theater set, performing Gioachino Rossini's *The Barber of Seville*. It's no wonder, then, that Martina Franca has become home to one of the most enchanting music festivals in Italy.

A group of local music lovers gave Martina Franca a whole new purpose in 1975. Supported by Paolo Grassi, who was director of the Teatro alla Scala in Milan in the 1970s, they founded the Festival della Valle d'Itria, an event that stands out among other summer happenings in Italy. The main focus of this festival, which runs from mid-July to early August every year, is the restaging of forgotten or rarely performed operas. The formula has proven successful to this day.

Under the Puglian skies, works by Italian as well as German and French composers are performed in the large courtyard of the Palazzo Ducale. Another venue is the picturesque courtyard of an old Fattoria, a large farm dating back to the eighteenth century, just outside town.

The city comes to life throughout the festival. During these summer evenings, people sit in the squares and outside bars until well into the night. After the concerts have finished, late at night, spectators head to the bars in the old town, which is lit up like a stage set.

A BAROQUE GEM

The baroque style typical of Southern Italy characterizes the old town, but in a rather subtle way and less exuberantly than in Lecce, for example. Flat and unadorned façades are decorated with opulent ornaments on portals and windows. All building openings and entrances are discreetly embellished, in a way that even appears attractive to contemporary visitors. The countless palaces, churches, houses, and workshops are interconnected like in an Arab kasbah. They form a harmonious picture, complete with corners and alleys, in which visitors can get lost for short

OPPOSITE: **THE PIAZZA MARIA IMMACOLATA IS THE AESTHETIC AND SOCIAL CENTER OF MARTINA FRANCA.** LEFT: **THE CITY IS PEPPERED WITH LAVISHLY DECORATED BUILDINGS.**

stretches of time while continuously encountering new surprises.

The elegant façade of the Basilica di San Martino, dating from the eighteenth century, is an architectural masterpiece typical of Martina Franca. The high relief above the main portal immediately captures the eye; it depicts Saint Martin riding on horseback while cutting his cloak in half. The basilica's interior is a genuine triumph of the baroque era.

TASTEFULLY DECORATED

Martina Franca's churches resemble one another a little. The reason for that phenomenon is that the city found its fortune through agricultural production, and it received a completely new look in the eighteenth century. Every single building, even the smallest, but above all the twenty noble palaces, was converted and redecorated following the taste of the times. Even the old-town residences of rich farmers, whose courtyards were still home to their animals, bowed to the new dictates of fashion. So even these commercial buildings look elegant in the eyes of today's visitors.

The Palazzo Ducale towers over the Piazza Roma with its palm trees and fountains. Murals adorn the halls. From Cathedral Square, you can walk along the narrow and almost perfectly straight main street—a traffic-calmed zone nowadays, like most of the old town—to the semicircular Piazza Maria Immacolata. Numerous cafés have opened up within its oval arcades. Worth a mention is Caffé Tripoli, which serves tempting sweet ice cream made from ricotta cheese with figs.

An overnight stay in a hotel in the middle of the old town is especially charming. When the last night owls have gone home, Martina Franca exudes an ambiance that could not be any more enticing. The same is true for the afternoon, when the whole of public life takes a siesta, which usually lasts from 2 p.m. to 5 p.m. It's the best time to let yourself be seduced by the enchanting charm of this old town.

TRULLI AND WHITE TOWNS

In the immediate vicinity of Martina Franca, there are some curious things to see: dotted over the Valle d'Itria, there are a number of trulli. These traditional buildings with conical roofs are still inhabited today and can be rented. Alberobello is a small town that consists almost entirely of these curious cone-shaped houses. In contrast, Locorotondo, with its intact and picturesque old center, towers as a uniformly white town over the trulli below, on a hill not far from Martina Franca. Tens of thousands of olive trees grow in the region, many of which are more than one thousand years old. The locally produced olive oil is an intense green color, has a strong flavor, and is indispensable for the hearty dishes of the rich traditional cuisine of Puglia.

LEARN MORE
Martina Franca: www.prolocomartinafranca.it
Festival della Valle d'Itria: www.festivaldellavalleditria.it

LECCE – THE ZENITH OF ARCHITECTURE

AN INTEGRATED WHOLE OF A BAROQUE CITY

A stroll through the old town is enough to understand where the term "Barocco Leccese" comes from. No other city in Italy has quite as many palaces, churches, and other buildings that are as lavishly decorated. A feast for the eyes!

The epitome of luxuriance: Santa Croce is considered the highlight of the typical Puglian style of baroque. The cathedral from the sixteenth century was perfected in the seventeenth century when it received its finishing touches through intricate and lush embellishments—to the extent that it looks almost like a sculpture. The façade around the beautiful rosette at the center is a masterpiece of the baroque decoration frenzy. There are mythical creatures, putti, and animals supporting window cornicing, and even the plain columns are adorned. Inside, the carved and gilded coffered ceiling from the first half of the seventeenth century dazzles the viewer.

How did this small town, of all places, come to appear like the stage set for a baroque opera? Complete with palaces and churches whose architects seemed to strive towards outdoing each other in terms of baroque exuberance?

THE CENTER OF THE SALENTO

The economic heyday of Lecce was between 1550 and 1750. At that time, the city became the political and administrative center of the Salento, the southern part of Puglia. From the mid-seventeenth century, Lecce, in addition, experienced an artistic boom when the city received its present-day look and its characteristic baroque appearance. It is not

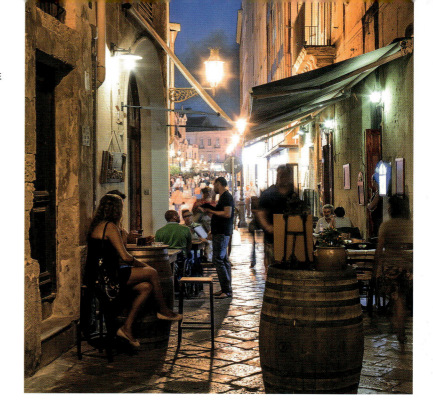

OPPOSITE: **THE BAROQUE STYLE COULD HARDLY BE ANY MORE PLAYFUL OR SKILLFUL: THE BASILICA OF SANTA CROCE.** RIGHT: **THE COMPLETELY RESTORED OLD TOWN IS A TRUE STAGE OF LIFE, ESPECIALLY AT NIGHT.**

without reason that Lecce was and is called the "Florence of the South." In terms of architecture and artistry, everything here seems like a uniform and integrated whole. Interestingly, a uniquely playful baroque style evolved in Lecce, a design barely influenced by Rome and Naples, the actual prime representatives of the Italian baroque.

The basic shape of the churches is an obvious example. In Rome and Naples, baroque churches feature curved shapes and façades and are based on oval floor plans. In Lecce, on the other hand, the façades keep their straight lines, and their lush adornment makes them look like gigantic reliefs. The floor plans resemble the shape of the Latin cross. Also typical of Lecce is that, although its architecture indulges in decorations and a love of form, the individual buildings never seem to lose their sense of elegance, lightness, and harmony.

BOUNDLESS DECORATIONS

In contrast to other old town centers of that time, such as in Martina Franca, everything in Lecce is geared towards a certain amount of excess. The motto here was: stop scrimping, start decorating. The result is just magical. The fact that Lecce missed out on economic booms in the nineteenth and twentieth centuries meant that the old town has remained almost completely intact, since there was never an urge to modernize or even to do away with the old.

The Palazzo del Governo is another magnificent example of the Barocco Leccese. Built in the mid-seventeenth century, its façade celebrates the baroque style from top to bottom. There are no plain surfaces void of embellishments. The façade of the church of Santi Niccolò e Cataldo is a curious sight. In the early eighteenth century, the Gothic portal was surrounded by a severe-looking façade that strived toward the sky and was crowned with abundant sculptural gems.

One important baroque building gives way to the next on Cathedral Square. The seminary, the cathedral, and a palace form a harmonious ensemble. Together, they make a perfect stage set to feed the desire for prestige of that time!

The Museo Provinciale Sigismondo Castromediano is home to a vast collection of Hellenistic and Roman artifacts from Lecce and its surroundings. In particular, the painted attic vases and bowls are among the most beautiful of their kind in the whole of Puglia. In the evening, when the sun that shines so brightly in the south slowly fades, the old town is illuminated and the magic of Lecce is revealed. Have an aperitif in front of a bar on a piazza—and you will feel like you are in paradise.

A LOT OF GOODIES

Lecce's baroque style is rich and abundant—and so is the local cuisine. "Ciceri e tria," pasta and beans, are a hearty classic. "Municeddhe" is the name of a snails dish, and "turcinieddhi" is a main course made from spicy goat entrails. Pasta lovers are in their element; the people of Lecce are convinced that their orecchiette pasta with tomato sauce is the best in all of Puglia. And then there are the "dolci," the desserts. For example, you simply cannot get enough of "fruttone," a flat cake with cream, almonds, and jam. The wine, of course, comes from the fields directly outside Lecce, as does the olive oil. A Garden of Eden for gourmets!

LEARN MORE
Lecce: www.infolecce.it

OTRANTO – PUGLIA'S MAGICAL SOUTH
AN AWE-INSPIRING FLOOR

There are only a few places in Italy that are famous for their flooring, and Otranto Cathedral is clearly one of them. But the village around the church is charming as well—and makes an excellent starting point for exploring the Salento.

The Salento is the southern part of Puglia. The heel of Italy's boot, it is an area that has been poor and run-down for centuries. This meant that very few of the old and important building structures were destroyed or modernized in the course of industrialization after World War II. Otranto is a good example of a small town in the Salento that still exudes the charm of an old port.

The town, which currently has fewer than 6,000 inhabitants, features a harbor that was an important trading hub for the merchants of Venice and Byzantium in the Middle Ages. On July 28, 1480, the fleet of Sultan Mehmed II, the feared ruler of the Ottomans, turned up here. He offered to spare the inhabitants of Otranto if they converted to Islam. The Christians refused. And so, after a two-week siege of the city, eight hundred of its citizens were brutally slaughtered and later declared martyrs in the Catholic Church. Their earthly remains—skulls and leg, arm, spinal, and pelvic bones, all in a big jumble—are exhibited to this day in large closets and glass cabinets in the cathedral's apsed chapel. An impressively terrifying sight!

MEDIEVAL SUITE OF IMAGES
Santa Annunziata, consecrated in 1088, is a key work of the Puglian Romanesque period. The basilica houses one of the most impressive works of sacred art of the European Middle Ages: its floor. The mosaic is enormous. More than ten million little pieces make up a work of art measuring 92 by 187 feet (28 by 57 meters) and covering an area of around 17,200 square feet (1,600 square meters). It was created by someone named Pantaleon, who was a monk known for

having been familiar with the myths and legends of Greece and also with those of the Northern European peoples. He translated more than seven hundred stories from the entire spectrum of European legends into the floor mosaic—a remarkable feature for a Christian church. Pantaleon created this work of art in just two years, between 1163 and 1165.

THE HEIGHT OF FANTASY

You simply cannot get enough of this pictorial carpet. There are elephants and camels, centaurs from pagan mythology, unicorns, leopards, and sirens luring sailors with their songs. The biblical Jonas is disappearing in the mouth of a whale, and the Queen of Sheba is entering with her court. A donkey is playing the harp, griffins and snakes make an appearance, club-swingers take part in a fight, and even a puss in boots features. You can marvel at the Garden of Eden, Noah, and the Flood, as well as the Tower of Babel, Alexander the Great, the symbols of the twelve months of the year, King Arthur, the virtues of man, hell, and paradise. In addition, the suite of pictures depicts tendrils and branches emanating from three large trees of life that spread out along the church floor in circles, featuring writing and ornaments. Visitors should take their time to dive deeper into this medieval world of legends and imagination. Every foot of the floor lets you see and discover more.

But there are further arguments for spending a night in Otranto. The romantic old town offers numerous cafés and restaurants right on the waterfront. In the fifteenth century, the Spaniards built the Castello Aragonese. Its defense towers provide a magnificent view of the city and the sea.

OPPOSITE: **IN OTRANTO, THE ENTIRE OLD TOWN WAS BUILT ON THE REMAINS OF GREEK AND ROMAN BUILDINGS.** *BELOW*: **ONE OF THE LARGEST, MOST UNUSUAL, AND BEST-PRESERVED FLOOR MOSAICS IN ALL OF ITALY IS THE FASCINATING CENTER POINT OF THE CATHEDRAL.**

AT THE TIP OF THE HEEL

From Otranto, a trip along the coast is a must. The road never strays far from the sea, all the way to the deep south. In Santa Maria di Leuca, the Adriatic meets the Ionian Sea. Here, Peter the Apostle is said to have come ashore and begun his missionary work, which led him all the way to Rome. Continue on the coastal road to Gallipoli. The intact old town, located on a peninsula, is surrounded by a mighty defensive wall. The Cathedral of Sant'Agata is an impressive example of Southern Italian baroque. Then, turn inland to travel back to Otranto—it's a perfect day trip!

LEARN MORE
Otranto: www.terredotranto.it
Gallipoli: www.gallipolitourist.it

DIAMANTE – THE PERFECT SEASIDE RESORT

THE NAME SAYS IT ALL

Diamante—"diamond"—is the name of this small town high above the Tyrrhenian Sea. It is part of the "Cedar Riviera," a coastal stretch of outstanding beauty that has—unbelievably—so far attracted very few vacationers.

Calabria may make one immediately think of the mafia, the so-called 'Ndrangheta. However, travelers will not come into contact with organized crime here. A tour into this region, which has still been largely ignored by foreign tourism, is free from danger.

On the west coast of Calabria lies Diamante, an exceedingly charming fishing village. Outstanding art and important historical buildings are few and far between. In contrast, the village of just under 5,000 inhabitants offers pretty hotels on the beach, cafés, and delicatessens with regional delicacies.

Diamante has a historical town center with a church dating from the late eighteenth century, and the "Lungomare," its promenade by the sea, is one of the most beautiful in Calabria. Murals are dotted all over the town; more than 150 of these works of art decorate the walls of people's houses. Diamante is popular with many Italian intellectuals as a summer retreat. The national poet Gabriele D'Annunzio, for example, often visited what he called the "Pearl of the Tyrrhenian Sea."

DISCOVERING THE CEDAR RIVIERA

Diamante is the ideal place to relax—and to explore the culinary delights of the Cedar Riviera. This part of the coast extends from Tortora to Paola. Most of the towns along this coastline are pleasantly void of tourists, such as Santa Maria del Cedro. The wonderfully sleepy village does not let on that its history dates back many thousands of years. The

OPPOSITE: SMALL, PRETTY, AND STILL MOSTLY A SECRET TO NON-ITALIANS: THE VILLAGE OF DIAMANTE. LEFT: MURALS ADORN MANY HOUSE WALLS HERE.

armies of Hannibal from Carthage are said to have passed by on their way to Rome.

Scalea is an attractive little town as well. Once you have passed the less charming newbuilds, the old town—full of nooks and crannies, as well as steep stairs and alleys that lead up to the Castello or down to the fine sandy beach—more than compensates. Places like these preserve the nostalgic charm of the 1950s and 1960s, which has long since disappeared elsewhere. It's Italy for insiders.

Since time immemorial, people have been cultivating a rare fruit on the 44-mile-long (70 kilometers) riviera, the rind of which is processed in many places. Citron fruit is a specialty for which Jewish people from all over the world travel here every year. The yellowish-green cracked rind smells refreshing and bitter. Citron fruit, also known as cedrate, is made into jams and liqueurs.

CITRON FOR SUKKOT

Jewish visitors are especially interested in the fruit itself. Rabbis look closely at the "etrog," the Hebrew word for citron, to choose only the most flawless fruits for the traditional bouquet for the Feast of Tabernacles. Why this fruit, of all things? According to the Jewish faith, the aromatic etrog is the fruit that Eve picked from the Tree of Knowledge in the Garden of Eden and passed on to Adam.

Every inhabitant of Diamante and the neighboring towns along the riviera is a citron connoisseur. And so visitors soon find out that the fruits most sought-after by Jews are those with a notch that resembles a bite. This notch is therefore called Adam's bite. Of course, local restaurants use cedrate for traditional dishes. For example, the rind is marinated in olive oil and garnished with roasted pine nuts. Very tasty!

THE HOME OF LICORICE

Almost a two-hour drive east of Diamante, on the Ionian coast of Calabria, lies Rossano. Here, a rare book treasure is kept in the Museo Diocesano: the Codex purpureus Rossanensis is considered one of the oldest gospels of all, with its 188 sheets with countless miniatures from the fifth and sixth centuries. San Marco Evangelista, a Byzantine-inspired church dating to the tenth century, is from the same period. But Rossano is also famous for its "black gold." The licorice produced here is considered to be the best in Italy. The company Amarelli Fabbrica di Liquirizia has been producing this jet-black delicacy since 1731. The factory is open to visitors.

LEARN MORE
Diamante: www.prolocodiamante.it
Rossano: www.rossanoturismo.it
Amarelli: www.amarelli.it

THARROS – THE ANCHORAGE OF ANTIQUITY

MULTICULTURALISM IN THE MEDITERRANEAN

The city's founders proved their good taste over 1,000 years BCE, and the geographical location of Tharros on the southern coast of the Sinis peninsula in western Sardinia is still fascinating. The fact that only ruins remain here today does not diminish its appeal.

Take a peninsula with the picturesque Gulf of Oristano on one side and the open Mediterranean Sea on the other. Build a city there, and you can kill two birds with one stone: the bay offers protection for merchant ships and fishing boats, and the inhabitants have a very charming place to live, surrounded on three sides by the deep blue sea. These, or something along those lines, may have been the considerations of the first people to set up their huts here in the thirteenth century BCE, on this peninsula on the western coast of Sardinia that, in parts, is only about 328 feet (100 meters) wide.

SARDINIA'S COMMERCIAL PORT NO. 1

Several centuries later, the Phoenicians sailed here from North Africa—today's Tunisia—and took full advantage of the location. They turned the settlement into a trading city. The magnificent ruins of a 394-feet-long (120 meters) pier at the harbor are evidence of just how significant Tharros was in the sixth century BCE. Here, multiple cargo ships could dock at once.

The Phoenicians were followed by the Romans, who stayed until the fifth century CE. During this time, Tharros changed fundamentally; wide streets, thermal baths, and theaters were created, as were a forum and the magnificent mansions of the local well-to-do. The excavated ruins give an idea of just how rich the city once was. It had a fully functioning sewerage system as well as water pipes to the private houses and thermal baths that are still clearly visible today. Many of the buildings directly on the coast show that even the ancient Romans preferred a home with a view of the sea.

OPPOSITE: **THE ANCIENT PORT CITY OF THARROS IS LOCATED ON A PENINSULA JUTTING OUT INTO THE SEA.** *LEFT*: **THESE ENIGMATIC GIANTS ARE THE ARTISTIC EXPRESSIONS OF A LITTLE-KNOWN PEOPLE.**

The ancient city, with roots in various centuries, is now part of the archaeological park. The excavations suggest that ancient Tharros must have been a fairly multicultural city. This isn't a surprise, since merchants from all over the Mediterranean docked here.

STEP BACK IN TIME

Among other things, gold from sub-Saharan Africa, Egyptian glass objects, and wine amphoras with stamps from Spain and southern France were found on the expansive grounds. Tharros was one of the most important places of transshipment for the entire island. No other excavation site in Sardinia can boast of such quantities of imported ceramics from various parts of the Roman Empire.

Touring around Tharros is like immersing yourself in more than two thousand years of architectural history, featuring ruins of the prehistoric Nuragic civilization, the first Phoenicians, the Romans, and the Byzantines. On view are the remains of fortified walls, Doric columns of a Greek-inspired acropolis, tombs of the necropolis including a sacrificial site, and the huge ruins of a Phoenician temple amid the bygone ancient city.

All of this is nestled in a breathtakingly beautiful landscape that invites you to linger, rest, and swim on the fine pebble "grain of rice" beaches—where people relaxed by the sea thousands of years ago.

HOTEL WITH A CERTAIN JE NE SAIS QUOI

A little under a two-hour drive away, situated directly on a wide beach and surrounded by dunes, is one of the most fascinating hotels in all of Sardinia: Hotel Le Dune Piscinas. The journey is worth it, because here, near the village of Piscinas, an old mine building from the nineteenth century has been transformed into a comfortable and truly one-of-a-kind hotel. The predominant sound here is that of waves crashing in the nearby sea. The hotel offers everything you need to spend entire days without contact with the stressful outside world. It's certainly not cheap, but it makes for a unique delight in Sardinia, and maybe even beyond.

LEARN MORE
Tharros: www.tharros.sardegna.it
Hotel Le Dune Piscinas: www.ledunepiscinas.com

BARUMINI – A WORLD HERITAGE SITE IN NATURE

SECRETS FROM THE DISTANT PAST

As the oldest village on the island of Sardinia, Barumini has another superlative feature: it is also the most mysterious. Located at the heart of the island, there are nuraghe buildings that hail from a prehistoric culture that only existed in Sardinia.

No one knows who the architects were. Nor does anyone know where they came from or what language they spoke. And so archaeologists called the inhabitants of Su Nuraxi, near the small village of Barumini, simply "people of the Nuragic civilization." They were closely related to the people of the Bonnanaro culture, which was widespread in Sardinia at the same time. A nuraghe is a building, and its legacy is the only key to this enigmatic culture. Each nuraghe is made of stones that have been piled up into conical shapes. Around seven thousand such nuraghes can be found all over Sardinia.

MYSTERY AFTER MYSTERY

What were these buildings used for? Archaeologists are still debating this too. The only thing that seems certain is that the buildings were erected between the second and first millennium BCE. Archaeologists suspect that they served a wide variety of purposes and were used as stables, residential buildings, and defensive structures.

Either a nuraghe towers on its own, usually atop a hill, or multiple are grouped together—as in Su Nuraxi, the largest nuraghe settlement in Sardinia, with an area of about 258,334 square feet (24,000 square meters). The settlement is so well preserved that it has been featured on the UNESCO list of World Heritage sites since 1997.

Su Nuraxi is dominated by one central nuraghe. It stands proud at a hill of about 46 feet (14 meters). The magnificent ruin is surrounded by a wall with four towers and a second circular wall. There are further nuraghes between these two wall rings. The entire village consists of the ruins and remains of about 150 such buildings. Experts believe that the central nuraghe used to measure 66 feet (20 meters), while the defense towers were up to 59 feet (18 meters) tall.

The nuraghes have small doors and window openings. Some of the windows face astronomical marker points, while most of the entrances face southeast. Another curious fact is that the almost always circular interior of these buildings was equipped with niches. What is their meaning? That remains a mystery, too.

Experts think that up to one thousand people lived in Su Nuraxi during its heyday. They also assume that the inhabitants were in contact with the builders of other nuraghes in Sardinia, because they all used similar construction methods. The nuraghes feature multiple stories inside and domed roofs on the outside. Just like with the trulli, exclusive to Puglia, the roofs of the nuraghes are also made of stones that are piled up without the use of mortar to form a tower that gets narrower towards the top.

A PROTECTIVE SPELL

Visitors can stroll through the narrow alleyways of the ancient village. The accommodation units, water reservoirs, and other buildings can be very

OPPOSITE: **IT REMAINS UNCLEAR TO THIS DAY WHAT PURPOSE THESE FASCINATING NURAGHES SERVED.** BELOW: **A GREAT NUMBER OF THE SEVEN THOUSAND NURAGHES FOUND ON SARDINIA ARE IN BARUMINI, SOME APPEARING LIKE VILLAGE STRUCTURES**

easily spotted. In the sixth century BCE, warriors from the North African Carthage destroyed the Nuragic civilization. In the following centuries, shepherds used these buildings to shelter their animals. The place was forgotten and considered by many to have had a spell cast on it, which proved fortunate because that meant its stones were never recycled into other buildings. Su Nuraxi is undoubtedly one of the most mysterious places on an island where many historical puzzles remain yet to be solved.

ANTIQUE SPA TREATMENTS

To the southwest of Su Nuxari lies the Antiche Terme di Sardara spa, already a famous resort in ancient times. The ruins of the Roman thermal baths are now part of a modern complex. The hot water and vapors help people with respiratory problems and skin diseases. The people of the Nuragic civilization apparently also knew about the water's healing properties. Not far from the ruins and the modern thermal baths, water spurts from the ground near the church of Sant'Anastasia. Inside the little church from the fourteenth century, there is another holy fountain, Pozzo sacro, from the Nuragic period, which gives reason to believe that the church was built above a pagan place of worship.

LEARN MORE
Barumini: www.fondazionebarumini.it
Antiche Terme di Sardara: www.termedisardara.it

STROMBOLI – A GREAT ISLAND SPECTACLE

VACATIONS ON THE VOLCANO

The island consists entirely of a volcano that is active 24/7 and often stirs at intervals of only a few hours or even minutes. That is just one of the reasons why a short break on its slopes, in one of the two island towns, remains an unforgettable experience.

A volcano that never sleeps. It can erupt again and again, 3,031-foot-high (924 meters) Mount Stromboli, to which the island owes its name. This miniature island only measures 4.9 square miles (12.6 square kilometers) in size. The whole island, which belongs to the Aeolian Islands, actually only consists of the volcano. The sides of this fiery mountain slope more or less gently into the deep blue of the Mediterranean Sea.

Although it is located in the middle of the sea, between the coasts of Calabria and Sicily, people settled here early on. In Roman times, the inhabitants of Stromboli did not only fish but also produced wine and olives. Almost three thousand people lived on Stromboli up until the late nineteenth century. But then, partly in the wake of volcanic eruptions and earthquakes, many people moved away, immigrating to the United States and Australia. Today, only about four hundred people live on the island.

THE SET FOR GREAT SPECTACLES

The island was rediscovered, if you want to call it that, through a movie. In 1949, Roberto Rossellini directed *Stromboli: Land of God*, his masterpiece of Italian neo-realism with Ingrid Bergman in the lead role. The directors Nanni Moretti and Vittorio de Sica also chose the fascinating natural scenery for their movies.

In the history of literature, "Stromboli" has always been synonymous with being far away from the real world. Jules Verne's novel *Journey to the Center of the Earth* ends here. Authors such as Alexandre Dumas and Friedrich Nietzsche mention the island in their works. They enticed travelers from the mainland, including many artists, writers,

OPPOSITE: WHEN THE LIGHT IS RIGHT, THE VOLCANIC ISLAND OF STROMBOLI IS PARTICULARLY ATTRACTIVE. *LEFT*: CARS ARE FROWNED UPON IN THE FEW DENSELY BUILT ISLAND VILLAGES.

actors, and politicians, who wanted to bid farewell to everyday life for a short time. People still want that today, but the journey does take a little bit of time and can only be done without your own car. Once there, you can rent an electric moped. The streets are narrow and bumpy; in many cases, the most elaborately restored and comfortably converted fisherman's cottages and farmhouses can only be explored on foot.

FANTASTIC VIEWS

On Stromboli, perfect peace, seclusion, and solitude are guaranteed. Many of the vacation and residential homes in the small villages of San Vincenzo and Ginostra are situated outside the town centers, high above the sea on the picturesque slopes of the volcano. The most bizarre spot on Stromboli is probably tiny Ginostra. The enchanting, secluded village can only be reached from the sea. Donkeys are still the only means of transport here.

You should only climb the summit of Mount Stromboli supervised by a guide. It's best done on a clear day when stunning panoramic views are guaranteed. It is highly recommended to book a hiking guide, as the ascent is not entirely risk-free. But it's worth the investment; you will never forget the view along the Sciara del Fuoco. When the volcano is more active, the lava flows from the crater along this "scar" directly into the sea. Whenever this is the case, the night sky is spectacularly illuminated.

The boat tours around the island, for example to Strombolicchio, are also memorable. This uninhabited neighboring volcanic island measures only approximately 3 square miles (8 square kilometers). Along a rock cliff rising steeply from the sea, a staircase with more than two hundred steps leads up to the lighthouse.

ISLAND HOPPING

If you worry you'd get lonely on Stromboli, you can visit the island on a day trip. There are good and regular ferry connections from the islands in the north and south. Lipari or other Aeolian Islands are more accessible for tourists than Stromboli. The seven islands of volcanic origin are home to comfortable resorts and luxurious hotels. Here, too, many cultural professionals have found a place to relax and be creative. Michelangelo Antonioni and the Taviani brothers made their films here, and Michael Radford immortalized the island Salina with his screen adaptation *The Postman*.

LEARN MORE
Stromboli and Aeolian Islands: www.eolie.me.it

THIS PAGE: **THE PIAZZA QUATTRO CANTI IN THE OLD TOWN OF PALERMO IS MESMERIZING IN EVERY DIRECTION.** OPPOSITE: **THE HUGE BAROQUE FONTANA PRETORIA MARKS A POPULAR MEETING SPOT.**

PALERMO – THE UNDERESTIMATED CITY
COMPLETE SPLENDOR

Goethe was swept away by Palermo. But later came the Mafia, and to this day, many travelers still do not dare to visit because they are afraid of the bosses. This is a big mistake, because this southern beauty does not warm the hearts of poets alone.

Goethe put it this way in his *Italian Journey* (translated by Alexander James William Morrison): "Italy without Sicily leaves no image on the soul; here is the key to all." And, one might add, Palermo is the key to Sicily. The capital of the autonomous region shares Naples' reputation as a metropolis visited only by a few Italy travelers for fear of the Mafia, known in Sicily since the nineteenth century as the Cosa Nostra. And, yes, in the 1980s and 1990s, the powerful bosses had unpopular prosecutors and politicians blown up, and even in the decades before then, everyone posing an obstacle to their activities was killed.

But numerous arrests and trials against the Mafia bosses and their staff have significantly weakened organized crime. And, importantly, the clans appear differently today—not as shooting gunslingers like in the movie *The Godfather*, but as perfectly dressed businessmen. Tourists need not be afraid of them any longer. They will not trouble travelers, so a visit to this immensely fascinating, surprising, and varied metropolis is a must.

The city can look back on a long and multifaceted history full of unexpected twists and turns, since, after all, Palermo was the capital of an Arab emirate for about two centuries. Those two

centuries have had an enormous impact on the city's architecture, culture, and everyday life.

A MIX OF CULTURES

It was the Phoenicians from North Africa who founded Pánormos in the seventh century BCE. They were followed in the third century BCE by the Romans and later by the Vandals. The Byzantine Empire also left its mark. The Arabs arrived in 831 CE and stayed until the early eleventh century. In 1072, the invading Normans, arriving from northern Europe, defeated the Arabs. These conquerors were followed by the Hohenstaufen dynasty with its legendary emperor Frederick II. He combined the Christian culture of the European Middle Ages with Arab influences in a historically unique way. He surrounded himself with Arab scholars who were among the world's elite and turned Palermo into a modern city for its time.

Angevin rule replaced the Staufers, and the French were eventually dethroned by the Spaniards. The capital of their empire, which encompassed all of Southern Italy, was no longer Palermo but Naples, where a Spanish viceroy governed. In the eighteenth century, the Austrian Bourbons took over, and it was only after the Italian unification in the middle of the nineteenth century that Palermo became an all-Italian city ruled by Italians.

At every turn, the visitor to Palermo encounters the influences of all these cultures, which made their mark on the city's history over about 2,500 years. Combined, these influences produced an inimitable style—in architecture, fine art, and even in the local cuisine. To name but two of many examples, two classic desserts in Palermo and Sicily are clearly influenced by Arabic culture: the wonderfully sweet and seductive "cassata" and "cannoli." An entire district in the historical center is still called the Kalsa, the Arabic word for "the chosen one." Most of the streets already existed in this way in the eleventh century, and many buildings were built on top of Arab buildings, which in turn were erected on ancient Roman ruins.

Palermo's old town is not particularly large and can be easily explored on foot. The Cathedral of the Assumption of the Virgin Mary is considered one of the most unusual sacred buildings in Italy. It was a mosque before being reconsecrated as a church. Arabic architectural influences are obvious on its façades and the apse.

GOLD, AS FAR AS THE EYE CAN SEE

Unfortunately, the interior was completely overhauled at the end of the eighteenth century, which means it lost much of its medieval character. Nevertheless, there are fascinating things to discover, such as the monumental sarcophagi made of valuable porphyry marble, containing the earthly remains of the Hohenstaufen emperors. The church treasure offers precious sacred art, some of its jewels inlaid with diamonds and rubies the size of a fingernail.

Not far from here is the Palazzo dei Normanni, which was built by the Normans in the eleventh century and became a meeting point for intellectuals from Europe and the Arab Empire during Frederick II's reign. There, something unusual awaits the visitor: the Cappella Palatina, which, together with the interior of the Cathedral of Monreale, is one of the only buildings in Italy whose walls are entirely decorated with mosaics on a golden backdrop. This total artwork was created in the eleventh century. Given the time of its creation, the images rather realistically depict stories from the Old and New Testaments. Medieval cloisters and Arabic domes harmoniously coexist in the church of San Giovanni degli Eremiti. Baroque

OPPOSITE: **THE VIEW ACROSS THE ROOFTOPS OF PALERMO HAS REMAINED LARGELY UNCHANGED FOR THE LAST TWO HUNDRED YEARS.** *TOP*: **THE PALAZZO DELLA ZISA IS A BUILDING FROM THE NORMAN PERIOD.** *BOTTOM*: **THE CAPPELLA PALATINA IS ALMOST COMPLETELY EMBELLISHED WITH MOSAICS ON A GOLDEN BACKDROP.**

decoration, on the other hand, triumphs in the nearby Chiesa del Gesù. The elaborately crafted marble inlays, which cover almost the entire interior, are particularly beautiful.

Baroque and Arabic architecture also combines in another unusual, yet harmonious way in the Church of Santa Maria dell'Ammiraglio complex. A church like this is unique in all of Italy. Built by the Normans, "La Martorana" received its exterior appearance in the seventeenth century. The bell tower is considered to be a masterpiece of Norman architecture.

The interior is slightly confusing, due to its abundance of murals from the eighteenth century, as well as precious and perfectly preserved mosaics from the Norman period. San Cataldo, right next to the campanile of La Martorana, was built during the Norman reign in 1160, yet this small church looks like a Turkish bath from the outside. Domes tower over the high walls. The interior still has the same rough charm as it did during the time of the Crusaders.

The Church of San Francesco di Assisi is nominally dedicated to the saint who preached poverty and modesty, but visitors will encounter here a church that is one of the most abundant in art in Palermo. Built in the thirteenth century, it is a kind of museum of religious art today, with works from the fifteenth to the eighteenth centuries. Just around the corner is a special architectural gem: the Oratorio di San Lorenzo from the late seventeenth century, which is lavishly decorated with stucco depicting allegories, sculptures, and magnificent reliefs.

BOULEVARD AND SHOPPING MILE

All of these places can be reached directly from the straight and elegant Via Marqueda, a boulevard with baroque palaces and churches, as well as monasteries, many stores, and restaurants. Where the Via Marqueda meets the Corso Vittorio Emanuele, all four sides of the buildings are designed as baroque fountains complete with abundant sculptures.

Palermo is also a city of magnificent aristocratic palaces, such as the Palazzo Abatellis from the late fifteenth century. It houses the Galleria

LEFT: **THE CHURCH OF SAN CATALDO SEEMS FAIRLY ORIENTAL.** *ABOVE*: **THOUSANDS OF MUMMIES AWAIT VISITORS IN THE CAPUCHIN CATACOMBS.** *OPPOSITE, TOP*: **IN THE BAROQUE COURTYARD OF THE PALAZZO NORMANNO LIES THE GATE TO THE CAPPELLA PALATINA.**

Regionale della Sicilia, an art gallery with key works by Renaissance and baroque painters, such as Antonello da Messina and Jan Gossaert. Impressively, the fresco *The Triumph of Death*, from the fifteenth century, covers an entire wall.

Many palaces are still privately owned, yet can be visited. One of the most magnificent villas with the best-preserved interior is the Palazzo Valguarnera-Gangi, featuring the famous hall of mirrors, a Rococo gem. This is where the ball scene in *The Leopard* by Luchino Visconti was filmed. Opera enthusiasts must not miss out on the Teatro Massimo from 1897. With a size of 83,205 square feet (7,730 square meters), it is the largest opera house in Italy.

ANCIENT BOYS AND DEAD MONKS

The ancient roots of Palermo are uncovered in the Museo Archeologico Regionale. Here, visitors will find true treasures, such as the sculptures from the Greek temples of Selinunte from the sixth century BCE and a famous ephebe, a bronze sculpture of a boy from the fifth century BCE.

There are two unusual places to visit in the south of the city that can be reached by taxi or on a charming walk. The Zisa, the Arabic word for "the splendid," is an elegant palace in the style of the Arab Fatimid rulers of the twelfth century. This country residence once belonged to an Arab paradise garden, which Normans, appreciative of art, had built. Not far away, visitors will find themselves in the realm of the dead. Below the Capuchin monastery are the catacombs of the monks. Here, thousands of deceased people were buried as fully clothed and embalmed corpses between the late eighteenth and early twentieth centuries. Like mummies, they stand and lie along several corridors—not unlike the ancient Roman catacombs—and stare at the frightened onlookers with empty eyes.

VUCCIRIA – PALERMO'S TUMMY

The Via Palermo and the Piazza del Garraffello mark the culinary center of the city. The so-called Vucciria had its origins in a twelfth-century meat market. Today, all conceivable kinds of food produced and harvested in Sicily are sold here. It is an extremely colorful, lively, and noisy market—which is why the word "Vucciria" is also used as a synonym for "chaos" in Palermo. On a walk through the market, which has been immortalized by painters like Renato Guttuso, visitors are presented with such an abundance of delicacies that you feel like tasting them immediately in one of the nearby restaurants. Among them are hearty local specialties, such as the typical street food dish of "stigghiola," the intestines of young sheep or goats, fried with salt and lemon juice.

LEARN MORE
Palermo: https://turismo.comune.palermo.it
Palazzo dei Normanni: www.federicosecondo.org
Cappella Palatina: www.cappellapalatinapalermo.it
Catacombe dei Cappuccini: www.catacombepalermo.it

MONREALE – DIPPED IN GOLD

A HEAVENLY CATHEDRAL

The Cathedral of Santa Maria Nuova towers like a fortress, with all of Palermo at its feet. This unique church is more than eight hundred years old, its interior is completely decorated with mosaics on a golden backdrop, and it has been a UNESCO World Heritage Site since 2015.

The infrastructure leaves a lot to be desired; there is only one regular bus service, which runs approximately every thirty minutes. A taxi ride there and back costs about 60 euros. For these reasons, a trip to Monreale is best done as part of an organized tour or by renting an inexpensive car. Why? The journey is definitely worth it, despite the fact that you have to calculate almost a half-day for this trip from Palermo. Even though there is only one church to visit in Monreale, this one is a stunner. In the truest sense of the word.

It was the Norman king William II—Guglielmo—of Sicily who laid the foundations for the cathedral in 1174, simultaneously with other representative buildings in Palermo. The ruler chose a place southwest of the city for his cathedral, on a hill overlooking the Conca d'Oro, the "Golden Valley." Once upon a time, there were only villas and orange groves here. Nowadays, there are also many illegally erected houses, but Palermo and the deep blue sea still provide a fabulous view.

A MOSAIC DREAM

The outside of the cathedral, including the two towers at the main portal, is almost plain, bar the apsis and the portal, which is decorated with a few mosaic inlays. The portal itself is a masterpiece of bronze art from the late twelfth century. The apse has an Arabic feel to it, with its many pointed blind arches and elegant inlays made of yellow, white, and black stone.

THIS PAGE: **THE ENTRANCE TO THE CATHEDRAL IS GUARDED BY NORMAN RULER WILLIAM II, THE KING AND FOUNDER.**
OPPOSITE: **THE CATHEDRAL BUILT BY THE NORMANS IN MONREALE, A FEW MILES OUTSIDE OF PALERMO, IS CHURCH ARCHITECTURE IN PERFECTION.**

Shortly before entering the church, you should take a deep breath—because what awaits you inside will simply take your breath away. The countless mosaics seem to topple over the visitor. Not a single surface is left undecorated. In only three years, between 1179 and 1182, artists from Constantinople, the capital of Byzantium, covered about 68,900 square feet (6,400 square meters) of wall space with mosaics. If you came prepared and have brought a small pair of binoculars or opera glasses with you, you will have a clear advantage. This is the only way to make out the many, quite realistically designed figures and landscapes that the artists created.

In the lower part of the church, the walls are covered with marble decorations, which, like the floor, date back to examples of Islamic art. After all, the Arabs ruled over Sicily for several centuries. Like Emperor Frederick II of Hohenstaufen, the Normans were seduced by the beauty of Islamic art and tried to integrate it into their representative buildings. The upper parts of the church walls are almost entirely embellished with mosaics in the Byzantine style. They show motifs on a bright golden backdrop that gives the interior a special glow on sunny days.

Like a comic strip, the individual groups of mosaic imagery depict scenes from Genesis and from the lives of Noah, Abraham, and other figures from the Old Testament. The life of Christ is recounted in the choir and the transepts. Many of the mosaics show lavishly detailed scenes from the Bible. For example, the depictions of Noah's Ark and the expulsion from Paradise resemble large

LEFT: THE COMPLETELY PRESERVED NORMAN CLOISTERED COURTYARD IS CHARACTERIZED BY ITS DIFFERENTLY DESIGNED COLUMN CAPITALS. *BELOW*: THE CHURCH ALSO FEATURES A RICHLY DECORATED BAROQUE CHAPEL. *OPPOSITE*: THE CATHEDRAL TOWERS OVER THE VILLAGE OF MONREALE LIKE A FORTRESS.

paintings rather than plain mosaics. The rich design leaves the viewer speechless in light of the artistry of the mosaic masters.

GIANT JESUS

The central apse features a huge Christ Pantocrator following the Byzantine model. This figure of Christ is 23 feet (7 meters) tall and 42 feet (13 meters) wide. The Mother of God is sitting on a throne beneath this giant figure, the Infant Jesus on her lap, accompanied by angels and apostles, all of them in front of a golden backdrop.

Because of the lavish decoration, the actual architecture of the cathedral initially fades into the background, though the church is an impressive example of the so-called Norman-Arab-Byzantine style. It has a stocky structure with large arches supporting the entirely wooden roof covering the interior, and the view into this open construction is fascinating. The side sections of these arches are also adorned with mosaics. Several aisles pass through the cathedral, through which visitors can access the upper floors and the roofs.

The cathedral treasure exhibits ritual objects, encased with jewels and gold. Yet it also features curious artifacts such as the chopped-off head of John the Baptist in its original size, its muscles and veins clearly visible along the open neck wound. The cloisters from the twelfth century, measuring 154 by 154 feet (47 by 47 meters), are particularly beautiful.

EXPANSIVE CLOISTERS

The cloisters also draw on Arabic influences, namely the pointed arches. They are supported by smooth and twisted double columns, which are also decorated with mosaic inlays. Visitors should take

their time to observe the column capitals, one after the other. Every capital is different. They feature fantastical flower and plant motifs as well as mythical creatures and groups of naked people, sometimes depicted in erotic scenes. For example, the capitals of one double column show a clothed man on the one side and a woman stripped to the waist on the other, whose full breasts are somewhat of a surprise in a church monastery. Christian and mythological beings come together here in a peculiar mix. One corner of the elegant cloisters is different from all the others: it forms a square courtyard with a fountain.

MONREALE'S SWEET TOOTH

After a visit to the cathedral, two nice cafés invite art connoisseurs to let themselves be seduced by sweet treats. On offer are cannoli, baked pastry shells filled with ricotta, chocolate, and candied fruit or with pistachio cream. Or "cubaita," a type of almond brittle with sesame and honey. Brightly colored confectioneries on small cookies or gelato, the local ice cream, replenish the calorie reserves. Not to mention "cassata," from the Arabic "quas at," which, in Monreale, is a cooled sponge cake with ricotta and candied fruit. Plus, there's the Arab "shariba," called "sorbetto" in Italian, a refreshing ice pop.

LEARN MORE
Cathedral: www.monrealeduomo.it

CEFALÙ – A CHARMING OLD TOWN BY THE SEA

A CATHEDRAL WITH A CLIFF BACKDROP

Many tourists in Sicily bypass the 14,000-inhabitant city fairly quickly or stop just for the cathedral. Yet this town offers wonderful walks and is a member of the so-called "club of the most beautiful villages in Italy."

On the northeastern coast of Sicily, Cefalù is situated beneath a huge cliff and nestled between a slope and the deep blue sea. People had already settled here in the fifth century BCE, and it's no wonder. The Tyrrhenian Sea is abundant in fish, and the Aeolian Islands to the north of Cefalù are ideal bases from which to explore it.

In 307 BCE, the Greeks conquered the village; about sixty years later, the Romans arrived. They created a network of straight roads, which, if you have a bird's-eye-view of Cefalù, is still visible today. After the fall of the Roman Empire came the Byzantines, the Arabs, and, in the late twelfth century, eventually the Normans. Some of the most important and beautiful buildings in Cefalù date from this period, when Arabic architectural and artistic elements were combined with Christian ones in a symbiosis unique to Sicily. Noteworthy, above all, is the cathedral, built by the Norman ruler Roger II. A church that recalls the Cathedral of Monreale in its mighty and imposing character, it is more of a fortified castle than a place of worship.

FROM THE MONASTERY TO THE PAWNBROKER'S

Just like in Palermo and Monreale, the entire apse of the cathedral of Cefalù is decorated with a huge mosaic on a golden backdrop, depicting a

OPPOSITE: A DOUBLY DREAMY LOCATION: CEFALÙ ON THE NORTHERN COAST OF SICILY IS NESTLED AT THE FOOT OF THE ROCCA. *LEFT*: EACH COLUMN IN THE CATHEDRAL CLOISTERS IS TOPPED BY A DIFFERENTLY SHAPED CAPITAL.

supernaturally large figure of Christ. Archangels and evangelists are on view here as well, preferably through small binoculars, which reveal the breathtaking details of the large-scale mosaics. The main church of Cefalù is complemented by a richly decorated and completely preserved cloistered court, with columns embellished with imaginative figures. Both the church and the cloistered court are listed as UNESCO World Heritage sites.

In the seventeenth and eighteenth centuries, the face of the old town changed. Several baroque churches and palaces were built, and older façades were adapted to the tastes of the times. A walk through the charming old town reveals many elaborately embellished building fronts. The pawnbroker's house, Monte di Pietà, dates from 1703. On the third floor of the building, you can view the original furniture of this institution. Even the old safe still exists, where pawned valuables were kept.

AN OFF-SHORE CRUISE

The best time to take a cruise off the coast of Cefalù is in the late afternoon. Around that time, the old town—with its former fishermen's cottages that line the shore—looks from the sea like a Nativity scene. Against this backdrop is a small but exquisite sandy beach. There are further coves to the west of the old town, almost all of which offer a magnificent view of Cefalù and the mountain massif behind it. This mountain range, the Rocca di Cefalù, reaches an altitude of around 886 feet (270 meters). Legend has it that Zeus, the father of the gods, transformed the nymph Daphne into this giant rock. This way, he saved her from Apollo's erotic pursuit—although nobody knows how Daphne felt about rescuing her honor in this way. On top of the Rocca range are the remains of a medieval castle dating from the fourteenth century.

HOTEL MUSEUM AND MUSEUM HOTEL

Art patron and hotel owner Antonio Presti has transformed the hotel by the sea he inherited from his father into a museum for contemporary art. Art is on display at the hotel Atelier Sul Mare—about a thirty-minute drive east of Cefalù in Castel di Tusa—not only in the lobby and in shared spaces. Internationally renowned artists such as Tano Festa, Fabrizio Plessi, and Pietro Consagra also designed the rooms and bathrooms. In some cases, guests have to adapt to these installations, which do not always provide the levels of comfort to which they might be accustomed. That's the price for experiencing a truly unique setting.

LEARN MORE
Cefalù: www.comune.cefalu.pa.it
Atelier Sul Mare: www.ateliersulmare.com

AGRIGENTO – A CLASSIC OF ANTIQUITY BY THE SEA

A TEMPLE WITH A VIEW

A field of ruins with Greek temples, from which visitors have a view down to the coast and to the sea toward North Africa: even the Italy traveler Johann Wolfgang von Goethe was enchanted by Agrigento's sophisticated symbiosis of architecture and nature.

At the end of April 1787, the almost forty-year-old privy councilor visited Girgenti, as he called the small town of Agrigento. Goethe was fascinated by the well-preserved temples, embedded in a green landscape with a view of the deep blue sea.

In the south of the town, which has little to offer except for the cathedral and the monastery of Santo Spirito, is the Valle dei Templi, the "Valley of the Temples," an archaeological park. In the sixth century BCE, the ancient Greeks built temples here as part of their town of Akragas. It developed into a rich trading town that was absorbed by the expanding Roman Empire in the third century BCE. It remained an important business location for trading relations between Sicily and the North African coast in the Middle Ages, but the temples fell into oblivion in the centuries that followed. When Goethe came here, a wild thicket surrounded the ancient buildings.

BETWEEN TOP CONDITIONS AND RUBBLE

In recent decades, "thanks" to widespread corruption, countless ugly newbuilds have been erected right up to the archaeological park. Unfortunately, they are difficult to overlook, but this does not detract from the beauty of the temples themselves.

The Temple of Concordia dates back to the early fifth century BCE. Together with the Temple of Hephaestus in Athens, it is the best preserved of

any Greek temple. It is a giant structure, spanning about 66 by 141 feet (20 by 43 meters) and almost 46 feet (14 meters) tall. Twenty steps lead up to the temple itself, with its columned hall consisting of six columns at the front and back and thirteen along either side, each of which is almost 23 feet (7 meters) tall.

The so-called Temple of the Dioscuri, from the mid-fifth century, was destroyed by an earthquake. In the nineteenth century, archaeologists reconstructed the northwestern corner of the temple from the original material found on site. Closeby is the completely collapsed, but very picturesque, Olympieion, the huge expanse of rubble from a temple that was built in celebration of the victory of the cultured Greeks over the barbarians—the Carthaginians. It was the largest Doric temple of Agrigento, with a footprint of 170 by 360 feet (52 by 110 meters). This temple used to feature huge sculptures. They measured around 26 feet (8 meters) in height and represented giants, legendary figures of Greek mythology. What these so-called "telamons" once looked like can be deduced from a sculpture that was reassembled, lying flat on the ground.

The Temple of Heracles is one of the oldest temple buildings in Agrigento. It once towered atop three-storied foundations. Its remains are spread far and wide across the grounds. Only eight columns still protrude into the azure skies of Sicily. At the beginning of the twentieth century, these were erected again to give visitors an impression of the complex on the former Porta Aurea.

ANCIENT PEOPLE'S ASSEMBLY

In the southeast of the plateau, where all these sacral buildings are located, are the ruins of the Temple of Hera from the fifth century BCE—another

OPPOSITE: **CONTEMPORARY ART AND MAGNIFICENT GREEK TEMPLES ENTER INTO A FASCINATING SYMBIOSIS IN AGRIGENTO.** BELOW: **THE TEMPLES ARE SURROUNDED BY LUSH GREENERY AND ARE NOT FAR FROM THE SEASHORE.**

Doric building with six by thirteen columns. It had already been reconstructed in Goethe's days. Today, twenty-three of the former thirty-four columns of the hall are standing.

The archaeological park also encompasses the ancient city walls and an early Christian necropolis, the early Gothic church of San Nicola, and an "ekklesiasterion" from the Hellenistic period. This is where the people gathered; around 3,000 citizens could sit here in twenty rows. The Museo Archeologico Regionale exhibits art treasures from antiquity and early Christianity.

INFINITE BEACHES

After so much antiquity, a dip in the sea is very refreshing indeed. And you need not drive far: over a stretch of 93 miles (150 kilometers), one fantastic beach follows another along coastal sections with few buildings and even fewer tourists. Like the Scala dei Turchi near Realmonte: a succession of dunes and sheltered bays, white beaches, and natural oases. One of the most beautiful beaches is Eraclea Minoa. It lies between the Platani River and the promontory of the Capo Bianco. Spiaggia di Giallonardo, Bova Marina, Capo Rossello, Cala Vicentina, and all the others: in these unspoiled bays, one can easily imagine what the ancient Greeks saw when they first set foot on Sicily.

LEARN MORE
Agrigento, Valle dei Templi: www.lavalledeitempli.it

PIAZZA ARMERINA – A VILLA CAUSES A SENSATION

A LEAP INTO ROMAN MODERNITY

The ancient Romans were more progressive than one might think. They were familiar with nudism, women's sports, and bikinis. The magnificent mosaics of the luxury Villa Romana del Casale are testament to that. It is located just outside the 21,000-resident city.

In the first half of the fourth century CE, a villa was built in the east of Sicily. It's a magnificent country house beyond compare, even in the context of the Roman Empire. It is not entirely clear who commissioned it, but whoever was able to afford the Villa Romana del Casale must have been exceedingly wealthy. The ruins of the house are not particularly noteworthy; the main focus is the floors of this noble or perhaps even imperial residence in the countryside, not far from the mountain village of Enna.

LOOK TO THE GROUND

Excavations in the past century unearthed about 37,674 square feet (3,500 square meters) of floor and wall mosaics. They are in keeping with the late Roman style—that is, a little less realistic than in the previous centuries of artistic glory. Many mosaics show geometric designs. The scenes depict people and celebrate the splendor, power, and lifestyle of the landlord and his family.

The North African influence on these mosaics is unmistakable. The Bardo National Museum in Tunis, Tunesia, exhibited magnificent large-scale mosaics that used to adorn the villas of owners of large Roman estates in today's Tunisia. The mosaic styles of these and the Piazza Armerina are so similar that archaeologists assume North African mosaic craftsmen were working in Sicily as well.

The motifs of this narrative image cycle rely on Greek mythology and Homer's epics. Visitors also get to see scenes from the luxurious everyday life of

OPPOSITE: **PLAN AN ENTIRE DAY TO VISIT THE HUGE MOSAICS IN PIAZZA ARMERINA.** *LEFT:* **THE LARGE AND LUXURIOUS ANTIQUE VILLA PROBABLY BELONGED TO A MEMBER OF ONE OF THE IMPERIAL FAMILIES.** *ABOVE:* **WOMEN IN BIKINIS DEMONSTRATE THE LIBERALISM OF ANCIENT ROME.**

well-to-do Romans, who seemed not to want for anything—not even in this provincial backwater, far from the capital, Rome.

EUROPE'S FIRST BIKINIS

The Roman state granted some freedom to women—especially those who were married to influential and wealthy men. They enjoyed liberties that women only regained many centuries after the fall of the Roman Empire. These included performing gymnastics in the open air, in extremely revealing clothing. Probably the most famous mosaic on this theme in Piazza Armerina depicts eight fit young women. Two of them are playing with a ball, and all of them are wearing bikinis, which draw attention to the ladies' fit physiques. The villa ostensibly did not belong to a Christian owner, because—with the advent of Christianity—women lost almost all of their liberties. This mosaic is of enormous importance for today's understanding of the role of women in the ancient Roman Empire.

Four areas of the large villa complex are currently open to visitors, including a monumental gateway with a horseshoe-shaped courtyard. The central body of the villa is clearly visible, extending around an inner courtyard where a garden blossomed in antiquity. There were three apses and, of course, a spa—the ladies in bikinis probably exercised and did their gymnastics there. The baths are also adorned with mosaics. There are several mosaics in the apartments reserved for the male members of the family. They quite clearly depict erotic scenes and figures such as Eros and Pan.

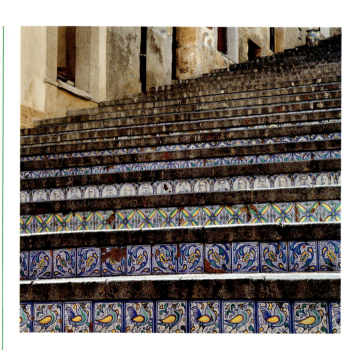

A TILED STAIRCASE

Those looking for the most beautiful ceramics in Sicily should embark on a thirty-minute drive from Piazza Armerina to Caltagirone. Rebuilt after the great earthquake of 1693, this charming town has been producing colorful and richly adorned ceramics for centuries. The 142 steps of the staircase leading to the church of Santa Maria del Monte are very charmingly embellished with ceramic tiles. The Museo Regionale della Ceramica has the whole gamut of this craft on display, featuring ceramics from the Norman period and Hohenstaufen dynasty, and above all imaginative pieces from the eighteenth century. Of course, you can buy ceramics in every corner of Caltagirone.

LEARN MORE
Piazza Armerina: www.villaromanadelcasale.it

THIS PAGE: THE ORTYGIA PENINSULA WAS CONSIDERED A CENTER OF CULTURE AND SCIENCE IN ANCIENT GREECE. *OPPOSITE:* IN RECENT YEARS, THE OLD TOWN OF SYRACUSE HAS BEEN COMPLETELY RESTORED, INCLUDING THE PALAZZO BENEVENTANO DEL BOSCO.

SYRACUSE – FROM POORHOUSE TO PRECIOUS CITY

BEAUTY AROUND EVERY CORNER

The historical center located on a peninsula of this southeastern Sicilian port town forms a world of its own. Thousands of years of history can be found in a small space. Since 2005, Syracuse and the necropolis of Pantalica have been designated UNESCO World Heritage sites.

According to the Greek poet Homer, the Sicels were engaged in the slave trade—at least that is how he represents them in the Odyssey. The fact is that before the Greeks, who settled on the east coast of Sicily near today's Syracuse in the eighth century BCE, the tribe of the Sicels lived here.

The Greeks populated the peninsula, which could be easily defended against attackers because of its strategic position, and called it Ortygia. They named their newly founded city Syracuse. Thanks to trade, it flourished to become the richest and most powerful city in Sicily in only a few centuries. And so it is no wonder that important Greek thinkers visited it too, including intellectual celebrities such as the philosopher Plato, the poet Aeschylus, and the all-rounder Archimedes, who invented sophisticated weapons of war to defend the city.

UNIQUE TREASURES

After the Greeks, the Romans set up camp, then the Byzantines, the Normans, the Habsburgs, and eventually the Italian Bourbons. Then, in 1861, Syracuse finally became part of a united Italy. In the first half of the twentieth century, the ancient city center fell into decline. Those who were able moved away. The fact that only the penniless remained here at that time seems completely incomprehensible nowadays. Completely restored to its former glory, the old town on the Ortygia peninsula now presents itself as a kind of open-air museum with magnificent buildings from various eras of the city's 2,500 years of architectural history.

Syracuse is home to unique treasures such as the Cathedral of Santa Maria delle Colonne. This church was built in the seventh century, inside the temple of the goddess Athena, which still existed at that time and dated back to the heyday of Greek rule. The Temple of Apollo is yet another one hundred years older and originated in the sixth century BCE. It is considered the oldest Greek temple in all of Sicily.

A walk through Ortygia is a journey through stage sets turned into stone, above all baroque in appearance. Dating from the seventeenth and eighteenth centuries are most of the palaces and churches, such as the Palazzo Bellomo. It houses the Galleria Regionale, the city's most important museum for ancient, early, and late medieval art, including two paintings that are among the most important in Italian art history. Antonello da Messina created one of the most beautiful Annunciations of Renaissance art in 1474, and painting genius Caravaggio's *Burial of St. Lucy* from 1609 also hangs here. St. Lucy is the patron saint of Syracuse.

A SOURCE BY THE SEA

Baroque palaces dominate the Piazza Duomo. Almost all of them were medieval fortresses before they were redesigned. The Palazzo Beneventano del Bosco was originally a fortified castle before it was converted into one of the city's most elegant buildings in the eighteenth century.

THIS PAGE: ALMOST ALL OF SYRACUSE'S HISTORICAL BUILDINGS ARE BUILT ON TOP OF ANTIQUE REMAINS, INCLUDING THE CATHEDRAL IN THE OLD TOWN. IT WAS ERECTED ON THE RUINS OF A TEMPLE. *OPPOSITE*: THE FOUNTAIN OF ARETHUSA IS PERHAPS THE CITY'S BIGGEST MIRACLE: A FRESHWATER SOURCE RIGHT BY THE HARBOR.

At the center of the peninsula, there was a hole that has since been walled in; the Fountain of Arethusa is a freshwater source just a few feet away from the sea. This is where, in antiquity, the nymph Arethusa—who was said to have lived here—was revered. What is certain is that the papyrus plants all around were mentioned by ancient authors.

The southern tip of the peninsula is occupied by the citadel Castello Maniace. The name goes back to a Byzantine general, a certain George Maniakes. With the help of Norman mercenaries, he reconquered Syracuse for the Byzantine Empire. Hohenstaufen Emperor Frederick II, a passionate builder, turned the medieval castle in the thirteenth century into a fort whose ruins still impress today.

THE NEW TOWN: TWO THOUSAND YEARS OLD

When the locals say "new town," they mean those districts that were erected on the mainland from the fifth century BCE onwards. Today, the Parco Archeologico della Neapolis is located there. The Greek theater, which was expanded by the Romans, is very well preserved: sixty rows of seats carved into the rock provided space for 15,000 spectators. Theatrical sea battles were put on in the amphitheater; at 459 feet (140 meters) long and 394 feet (120 meters) wide, it could be completely flooded with water. The ruler Hieron II's altar of sacrifice was also enormous: almost 656 feet (200 meters) long, 72 feet (22 meters) wide, and 36 feet (11 meters) high, complete with two ramps over which more than four hundred sacrificial animals were led on holidays.

Located in the archaeological park are the so-called Latomies, ancient limestone quarries. In one of the limestone rocks, the Greeks had the "Ear of Dionysius" carved. This artificial cave is over 197 feet (60 meters) long, 36 feet (11 meters) wide, and about 65 feet (20 meters) high. Anyone who speaks or even just whispers deep inside this cave can be understood perfectly on the outside, through an acoustic effect that still fascinates visitors today.

In the new town, the church San Giovanni Evangelista was built in the fourteenth century. The great earthquake of 1693 destroyed the place of worship. Among the preserved ruins is the crypt of Saint Marciano, supposedly a disciple of Paul the Apostle. In 44 CE, he was said to have founded the first Christian parish in Syracuse, and he later became the parish's first bishop. Legend has it that Saint Peter himself preached at the altar of the crypt. The crypt leads into an extensive catacomb system, which is the largest in Italy after the underground tombs of Rome.

GREEK MEGA FORTRESS

In the fourth century BCE, Dionysius I had a mighty fortress built on the highest elevation near Syracuse, today about 4.3 miles (7 kilometers) outside the city. Its magnificent ruins continue to fascinate. Castello Eurialo was able to house more than 3,000 soldiers and 400 riders, plus their horses, making it one of the most important fortifications of Greek antiquity in the whole Mediterranean. Secret passages underground connected the fortress with the ancient city by the sea. This is allegedly where Archimedes employed his burning mirrors, using the sun to set fire to the sails of the enemy's ships.

LEARN MORE
Syracuse: www.siracusaturismo.net
Parco Archeologico della Neapolis: www.regione.sicilia.it

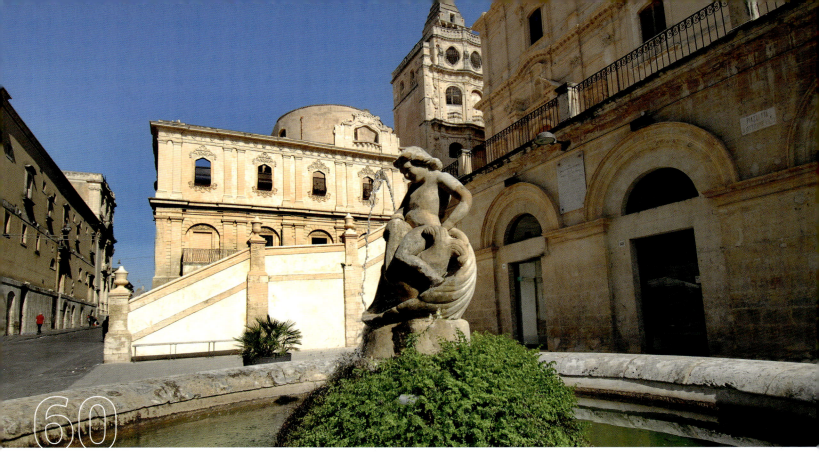

NOTO – RISEN FROM THE ASHES

A BAROQUE DREAM

Like phoenix rising from the ashes, this small town on the southern coast of Sicily reinvented itself after a catastrophic earthquake and was rebuilt completely in the baroque style typical of the island. The picture-perfect city has an awe-inspiring number of beautiful churches.

On January 11, 1693, the earth trembled—so much so that Noto, a small town in the province of Siracusa, was destroyed. The devastation was so great that people decided to let the ruins be ruins. The old Noto is now buried under vegetation. The new Noto was built according to then modern rules of urban design; the result is a baroque oasis, surrounded by farmland and livestock.

A local nobleman, Giuseppe Lanza, Duke of Camastra, was responsible for ensuring that the urban planning principles of the late seventeenth and early eighteenth centuries were applied to an entire town. This ambitious project was the first of its kind in Southern Italy. Even today, the streets and expansive squares of Noto are still arranged on a grid pattern. Everything here seems somehow modern and following a rational pattern; narrow and winding alleys were to be avoided at all cost. Nevertheless, individual buildings, especially grand churches and palaces, were allowed playful elements. By achieving this balancing act, Noto became the undisputed capital of the Sicilian baroque, whose desire for decoration did not stop at monsters and hybrid creatures of half-man, half-animal.

PALACES LIKE PEARLS ON A STRING

The Corso Vittorio Emanuele is Noto's main artery. Several baroque palaces of the local aristocracy tower over the boulevard. Each family seemingly wanted to outdo the next when it comes to lavish embellishments.

OPPOSITE: ALMOST THREE DOZEN CHURCHES SERVE THE 24,000 INHABITANTS OF NOTO—FOR EXAMPLE, SAN FRANCESCO D'ASSISI ALL'IMMACOLATA. LEFT: VOID OF NEWBUILDS, THE OLD TOWN HAS BEEN ABLE TO EXUDE A VERY SPECIAL CHARM TO THIS DAY.

Located on the Corso is the church of San Francesco d'Assisi all'Immacolata from the first half of the eighteenth century. Opposite this elegant church is Santa Chiara, with its oval interior.

The main square of Noto is the Piazza del Municipio. The buildings that line it constitute a kind of catalog of Sicilian baroque architecture. Visitors get to see all conceivable decorative elements of the time, all in a single place. And there is, of course, also a prestigious church: the cathedral, which is a late baroque work. In 1996, the mighty dome collapsed. In 2016, restorations were completed and the cathedral reopened. The perfectly straight Via Nicolaci looks like the stage prop for a Mozart opera, with elegant townhouses and palaces, one after the other. The balconies deserve a special mention. Many are supported by sculptures that depict grotesque and fearsome figures.

A FIVE-DOMED CHURCH

One of the most successful—read: most elegant—examples of Sicilian baroque is San Domenico, consecrated in 1727. It has an impressive five domes. The Via Cavour is yet another triumph in terms of baroque residences, churches, and monasteries.

Noto must have had an active social life in the eighteenth and nineteenth centuries, with numerous noble and patrician families visiting the theaters and leaving their elegant mark on the city. Not much of this is still felt today; Noto is a small, provincial town. Still, it exudes plenty of charm, and staying overnight is certainly recommended. After dark, the illuminated old town reveals its most beautiful side.

MODICA – LIKE A NATIVITY SCENE

In 1693, Modica—about 22 miles (35 kilometers) west of Noto—was also destroyed and subsequently rebuilt. Right in the middle of the city is San Giorgio Cathedral, an imposing baroque church with an elegant staircase leading up to the house of God. Modica is at its most beautiful just before sunset, when the town built on a slope—with its narrow, crisscrossing alleys and densely built houses—looks like a huge illuminated Nativity scene. Modica is famous for its excellent chocolate, such as the offerings from the chocolaterie Antica Dolceria Bonajuto, which has been in operation since 1880. The top restaurant, Accursio, which has a Michelin star, also uses local chocolate on its menu.

LEARN MORE
Noto: www.siracusaturismo.net
Antica Dolceria Bonajuto: www.bonajuto.it
Accursio: www.accursioristorante.it

THE DOME OF THE CATHEDRAL OF NOTO COLLAPSED NEAR THE END OF THE TWENTIETH CENTURY, BUT IT HAS SINCE BEEN RESTORED TO ITS FORMER GLORY.

INDEX

Agrigento 148, 178–9
    Valle dei Templi 178–9
Alberobello 153
Alberti, Leon Battista 38
Aosta 14–15
    Arch of Augustus 14–15
    Teatro Romano 14
Aquileia 22–3

Barga 75–6
Barumini 162–3
Bassano del Grappa 20–21
    Bridge 21
    Convento dei Minori 20
Bertolucci, Bernardo 39, 83
Bologna 9, 53, 60, 75
    Piazza Maggiore 62–3
    San Petronio 62
    Torre degli Asinelli 63
    Torre Garisenda 63
Bomarzo 106–7
Brescia 24–5
    Complesso di Santa Giulia 25
    La Rotonda 24
    Pinacoteca Tosio Martinengo 24–5

Caprarola 9, 112–3
    Palazzo Farnese 112–3
Caravaggio 57, 142–3, 184
Caserta 132
Castel del Monte 137
Castello Eurialo 185
Cedar Riviera 158
Cefalù 176–7
Cimabue 64
Civita di Bagnoregio 9, 104–5
Como 18–19
    Brunate 19
    Cathedral 18
    Casa del Fascio 19
    Sant'Abbondio 18
Cori 129
Cosmati 109–10

Dante Alighieri 69, 76, 82–3
Diamante 158–9

Eco, Umberto 17
Eyck, Jan van 31

Farnese, Alessandro 112–3
Ferrara 48
    Castello Estense 51
    Palazzo di Ludovico il Moro 50
    Palazzo Schifanoia 50

Flora, Paul 13
Francesca, Piero della 49, 80
Frederick II 137, 168–9, 174, 185

Gallipoli 157

Genoa 54, 71
    Aquarium 58–9
    Cattedrale di San Lorenzo 58
    Palazzo Bianco 57
    Palazzo Doria Pamphilj 57
    Palazzo Ducale 57
Giardino Spoerri 90–1
Giotto 53, 64
Glurns 12–13
    Mals 13
    Saint Pankratius 12
Gressan 15
Gubbio 84
    Corsa dei Ceri 86
    Palazzo dei Consoli 86
    San Francesco 86–7

Hemingway, Ernest 28–9
Herculaneum / Ercolano 144
    Villa dei Papiri 146
    Terme Suburbane 147

Juvarra, Filippo 18, 31–2, 38

La Verna 76–7
Lecce 152, 154–5
    Barocco Leccese 154–5
Liparian Islands 165
Locorotondo 153

Mantegna, Andrea 38, 51, 143
Mantua 36
    Palazzo del Te 39–40
    Palazzo Ducale 36–7
    Teatro Scientifico 37–8
Marina di Leuca 157
Martina Franca 152–3, 155
    Festival della Valle d'Itria 152–3
    Trulli 153, 163
Matera 150–1
Menotti, Gian Carlo 95
Michelangelo 8, 33, 102–3, 143, 165
Modica 187
Monreale 169, 172, 176
da Montefeltro, Federico 79, 87
Montagnana 42–3
Montefiascone 105
Monteriggioni 72–3, 82–3
Mussolini, Benito 19, 146

Naples 9, 133, 138, 145, 155, 167–8
    Cappella Sansevero 141
    Catacomba di San Gennaro 143
    Certosa di San Martino 142
    Dom San Gennaro 141–2
    Museo Nazionale della Ceramica 142
    Palazzo Reale 140
    Sanità 143
    Spanish Quarter 138, 142–3
    Teatro San Carlo 138
Ninfa 128–9
Noto 9, 186

Orsygna 74–5
Orta San Giulio 16–17
    Isola San Giulio 16–17
    Sacro Monte 17
Orvieto 100
    Cathedral 101–2
    Museo dell'Opera del Duomo 103
    Pozzo di San Patrizio 101, 103
Ostia Antica 124
    Amphitheater 126
    Forum 125–6
    Synagogue 127
    Tempio Rotondo 126
Otranto 9, 156–7

Paestum 148–9
Palermo 166, 172, 176
    Cappella Palatina 169, 171
    La Martorana 169–70
    Palazzo Abatellis 171
    Palazzo Valguarnera-Gangi 171
    San Cataldo 170
    San Francesco d'Assisi 170
    Teatro Massimo 171
    Zisa 171
Palestrina 122–3
    Palazzo Colonna Barberini 123
Palladio, Andrea 21, 24, 43
Pantaleon 156–7
Parco dei Mostri 106–7
Parma 44
    Cathedral 46–7
    Teatro Regio 44
    San Giovanni Evangelista 47
Pavia 34–5
    Certosa di Pavia 34–5
    San Michele 35
Phlegraean Fields 143
Piazza Armerina 180–1
    Villa Romana del Casale 180–1
Piscinas 161
Pitigliano 98–9
    Via Cave 99
Pomposa 52–3

Ravenna 52–3, 66, 85
    Sant Apollinare in Classe 69
    Sant Apollinare Nuovo 68–9
    San Vitale 66–7
Reggia di Caserta 133
Rome 8–9, 116
    Basilica di San Vitale 121
    Baths of Caracalla 119
    Catacomba di Santa Priscilla 119
    Cloaca Maxima 120
    Domus Romana di Palazzo Valentini 118, 120
    Domus Romane del Celio 120
    Excubitorium 120
    Ipogeo di Via Livenza 118
    Mitreo del Circus Massimo 116
    Mitreo di Santa Prisca 116

Vatican 9, 119–20
Vicus Caprarius 119
Roncole Verdi 47
Rossano 159
Rossellini, Roberto 164

Sacro Bosco 106–7
San Clemente a Casauria 114–5
San Galgano 88–9
San Leo 81
San Leucio 135
Sant'Antimo 91
Santi, Raphael 39, 80–1, 113, 143
Scala dei Turchi 179
Scalea 159
Signorelli, Luca 102–3
Spoerri, Daniel 90–1
Spoleto 94
    Festival dei Due Mondi 95
    Fonti del Clitunno 97
Stromboli 9, 164–5
Su Nuraxi 162–3
Syracuse 182
    Ear of Dionysius 185
    Palazzo Beneventano del Bosco 184–5
    Parco Archeologico della Neapolis 185
    Santa Maria delle Colonne 184

Tarquinia 110–1
    Lido di Tarquinia 111
    Necropolis 110–1
Terme di Petriolo 89
Terme di Sardara 163
Terzani, Tiziano 74–5
Tharros 160–1
Tiepolo, Giovanni Battista 20, 35, 47
Titian 25, 27, 57, 81
Torcello 28–9
    Santa Maria Assunta 29
Trani 136–7
Treviso 26–7
    Museo Civico Luigi Bailo 27
    San Nicolò 26
Triora 70–1
Turin 9, 18, 30
    Cathedral 31–7
    Chapel of the Holy Shroud 32
    Mole Antonelliana 32
    Museo Civico d'Arte antica 31
    Palazzina di Caccia di Stupinigi 32
Tuscania 108–9
    San Pietro 108–9
    Santa Maria Maggiore 108–9

Uccello, Paolo 81
Urbino 78, 85
    Casa Natale di Raffaello 81
    Palazzo Ducale 80–7
    San Giovanni Battista 81

Vesuvius 142, 147

PHOTO CREDITS

INTERIOR:

Huber Images: p. 1, 89 top, 187 center (Guido Cozzi); 2–3, 84, 94, 95, 96, 155 top (Maurizio Rellini); 4 left, 13 top, 129 center (Udo Bernhart); 7, 8, 172, 174 right, 177 center (Antonino Bartuccio); 9 top, 21 bottom, 51, 67 (Gabriele Croppi); 10–11, 57, 99 top right (Matteo Carassale); 13 bottom (Frank Lukasseck); 21 top (Colin Dutton); 23 top, 28, 66, 100, 110, 132 (Guido Baviera); 23 bottom, 83 top (Stefano Scatà); 29 top, 114, 115 bottom, 153 center, 182 (Johanna Huber); 36 (Luigi Vaccarella); 37 (Mark Robertz); 38 (Marco Arduino); 43 center (Stefano Renier); 44, 146 right (Massimo Ripani); 48 (Monica Goslin); 60, 120 top (Pietro Canali); 65 (Stefano Torrione); 72–73 (Douglas Pearson); 80 left (Günter Gräfenhain); 81 (Olimpio Fantuz); 90, 107 center (Ferruccio Carassale); 98, 137 center, 160 (Riccardo Spila); 105 top (Franco Cogoli); 105 bottom (auralaura); 111 top left (Zoltan Nagy); 113 top, 124 (Angelo Giampiccolo); 130–131, 151 top, 158, 159 top (Arcangelo Piai); 134 left, 149 center, 171 top (Giovanni Simeone); 134 right (Giuseppe Dall'Arche); 142 right, 157 top, 166, 184 left (Massimo Borchi); 146 left (Giorgio Filippini); 157 bottom (Ugo Mellone); 163 top (Christian Bäck); 164, 180 (Alessandro Saffo); 165 top (Manfred Bortoli); 169 top; 170 left (Luca Scamporlino); 174 left (Marco Simoni); 181 center (Sabine Lubenow); 184 right (Colin Dutton)

Lookphotos: p. 25 top (Friedel, Alex Tino); 49, 68 right, 153 top (Stankiewicz, Thomas); 50 right, 144, 148, 177 top, 185 bottom (age fotostock); 56 left (Johaentges, Karl); 76, 77 bottom (Richter, Jürgen); 86 (ClickAlps); 91 top (Maeritz, Kay); 141 top, 173 (robertharding); 162 (Lengler, Gregor); 175 top (Martini, Rainer)

Shutterstock: p. 4 center, 106, 150 (canadastock); 4 right (leoks); 5 center (Cardaf); 5 right (Alessandro Cristiano); 9 center (Gennaro Leonardi); 12 (Chris Rinckes); 14 (escapetheofficejob); 15 top (SerFeo); 15 bottom (jakubtravelphoto); 16 (pcruciatti); 17 top (Isogood_patrick); 17 bottom (Cristian Puscasu); 18 (Heracles Kritikos); 19 top, 32 right (Claudio Divizia); 19 center (KucherAV); 20 (Yasonya); 22 (Pecold); 24 (BNFWork); 26, 27 top (Velishchuk Yevhen); 27 bottom (Elena Rostunova); 29 bottom (TMP - An Instant of Time); 30 (Roberto Lusso); 31 (iacomino FriMAGES); 32 left (EnricoAliberti ItalyPhoto); 33 (Lois GoBe); 34 (Mate Karoly); 35 bottom (lorenza62); 35 top (Adam Jan Figel); 39 top (Mor65_Mauro Piccardi); 39 center (Alberto Masnovo); 40–41 (spatuletail); 42 (Ditlevsen); 43 top (makalex69); 45 (cge2010); 46 center (Wanessa_p); 46 bottom (iryna1); 47 (foundfootage); 50 left, 52, 53 top (Gaia Conventi); 53 bottom (Edoardo Bonetto); 54 (Luca Rei); 55 (lindasky76); 56 right (Davide Scio); 58 (Boris Stroujko); 59 top (Christian Vinces); 59 center (ArTono); 61 (Akhenaton Images); 62 left (milosk50); 62 right (Joost Adriaanse); 63 (vvoe); 64 left (cge2010); 64 right (Massimo Parisi); 68 left (Dmytro Surkov); 69, 178, 188–189 (javarman); 70 (leoks); 71 left (Winnie Ho); 71 right (kuvona); 75 top (Mauro Pezzotta); 75 bottom (Travelvolo); 77 top (GoneWithTheWind); 78 (tokar); 79, 151 bottom (Gimas); 80 right (trotalo); 82 (GagliardiPhotography); 83 bottom (Federico Magonio); 85 (spatuletail); 87 left (Buffy1982); 87 right (Marco Falcini); 88 (ER_09); 89 center (s74); 91 center (Simone Crespiatico); 92–93, 99 center, 104 (ermess); 97 (Stefano_Valeri); 99 top left, 101 (ValerioMei); 102 left (Boris Stroujko); 102 right (Karta-Ivrea); 103 top (Boris Stroujko); 103 center (sdesa89); 107 top (Ragemax); 108, 109 top (Lucky Team Studio); 109 center (robertonencini); 111 top right (Takashi Images); 111 center (Alessio Stefanoni); 112 (bruno pagnanelli); 113 center (Claudio Caridi); 115 top (underworld); 116 (Peeradontax); 117 (ariy); 118 (Kirk Fisher); 119 top (marcovarro); 119 center (Sun_Shine); 121 (BestPhotoStudio); 122 (Bruno Arena Fotografie); 123 top (Stockafisso); 123 bottom (Giancarlo Polacchini); 125 (Dimsle); 126 (Juan R. Velasco); 127 top (Alberto Masnovo); 127 center (tilted.angle); 128 (LifeCollectionPhotography); 129 top (Alessandro Tortora); 133 (kaprik); 135 (auralaura); 136 (Alexandre G. ROSA); 137 top (Emily Marie Wilson); 138 (iacomino FriMAGES); 139 (marcobrivio.photo); 140 (lazyllama); 141 bottom (Sergey_Bogomyako); 142 left (BrunoRosa); 143 top (Inu); 143 center (Peter Schwarz); 145, 147 top (WitR); 147 center (Vaclav Volrab); 149 top (Dietmar Rauscher); 152 (David Ionut); 154 (DeltaOFF); 155 bottom (Massimo Todaro); 156 (Alexandre G. ROSA); 159 center (Antonio Gravante); 161 top (Savazzi Photo); 161 center (Elisa Locci); 165 center (maudanros); 167, 179 top (Romas_Photo); 168 (marcociannarel); 169 center (Kiev.Victor); 170 right (Stanislavskyi); 171 bottom (Chris Lawrence Travel); 175 bottom (a9photo); 176 (kavalenkava); 179 bottom (maudanros); 181 top left (Fabio Michele Capelli); 181 top right (luigi nifosi); 183 (Keith Hider); 185 top (Michele Ponzio); 186 (EnricoAliberti ItalyPhoto); 187 top (spatuletail)

Mauritius Images: p. 74 (Alamy / TCD/Prod.)

Photographic Archives Museums of Brescia – Fotostudio Rapuzzi: p. 25 center

Thomas Migge: p. 109 bottom, 120 center

Sergio Melis: p. 163 bottom

Front Cover: Located on a steep cliff: Civita di Bagnoregio (shutterstock/Nikiforov Alexander)

Back Cover: *top left*: From the hills, you have a fantastic view of Turin and the Alps (Shutterstock/ Doctor_J); *top center*: Hills and vineyards in the fall, province of Treviso (Arcangelo Piai/HUBER IMAGES); *top right*: Treviso is Venice in miniature without mass tourism but with much local color (Massimo Borchi/HUBER IMAGES); *bottom*: The old town of Bassano and the Ponte Vecchio seem like a picturesque theater set (Shutterstock/Yasonya).

Page 1: Tuscania: The ruins of the fortress and the church of San Pietro (Guido Cozzi/ HUBER IMAGES).

Pages 2–3: Enchantingly illuminated: the cathedral and town of Orvieto (Maurizio Rellini/ HUBER IMAGES).

ABOUT THE AUTHOR:

Thomas Migge, born in Hagen, Germany, has chosen Italy as his home for almost thirty years. The passionate travel author and political correspondent writes for newspapers and magazines and is the author of numerous illustrated books.

Other Schiffer Books on Related Subjects:
Secret Cities of Europe: 70 Charming Places Away from the Crowds.
By Henning Aubel. 978-0-7643-6289-7

Secret Places: 100 Undiscovered Travel Destinations around the World
Edited by Jochen Müssig. 978-0-7643-6367-2

Copyright © 2023 by Schiffer Publishing, Ltd.
Translated from the German by Rebecca DeWald.
Originally published as *Secret Citys Italien: 60 charmante Städte abseits des Trubels.*
© 2021 Bruckmann Verlag GmbH, Munich, Germany

Layout: Octaviz Studios, Tanja Clauss
Cover Design: Regina Degenkolbe
Cartography: Huber-Kartographie, Heike Block

All information contained in this work has been carefully researched and updated by the authors and checked by the publisher. However, we incur no liability for the correctness of the information, and thus use is at your own risk. If this work contains links to third-party websites, we take no responsibility for their contents nor do we assume liability for them.

Library of Congress Control Number: 2022944478

All rights reserved. No part of this work may be reproduced or used in any form or by any means—graphic, electronic, or mechanical, including photocopying or information storage and retrieval systems—without written permission from the publisher.

The scanning, uploading, and distribution of this book or any part thereof via the Internet or any other means without the permission of the publisher is illegal and punishable by law. Please purchase only authorized editions and do not participate in or encourage the electronic piracy of copyrighted materials.

"Schiffer," "Schiffer Publishing, Ltd.," and the pen and inkwell logo are registered trademarks of Schiffer Publishing, Ltd.

Type set in TheSerifB/Stone Sans II

ISBN: 978-0-7643-6591-1
Printed in India

Published by Schiffer Publishing, Ltd.
4880 Lower Valley Road
Atglen, PA 19310
Phone: (610) 593-1777; Fax: (610) 593-2002
Email: info@schifferbooks.com
Web: www.schifferbooks.com

Schiffer Publishing's titles are available at special discounts for bulk purchases for sales promotions or premiums. Special editions, including personalized covers, corporate imprints, and excerpts, can be created in large quantities for special needs. For more information, contact the publisher.